DID HE SAVE
LIVES?

DID HE SAVE LIVES?

A Surgeon's Story

DAVID SELLU

Sweetcroft Publishing

First published in 2019 by
Sweetcroft Publishing

PB 978-1-912892-32-7
eBook 978-1-912892-33-4

Project management by whitefox
Designed and typeset by seagulls.net
Cover design by Madeline Meckiffe

Printed and bound in Great Britain by Clays Ltd,
Elcograf S.p.A.

For Ivy and Finlay,
The latest members of our family

'Everything we know in aviation, every rule in the rule book, every procedure we have, we know because someone somewhere died ...'

– Captain Chesley Sullenberger, the pilot who averted a catastrophe by landing his plane in an emergency on the Hudson River in New York, 2009

Preface

Recent high-profile cases have brought the relationship of medicine and law into sharp focus. I remember very clearly the moment I heard that a colorectal surgeon had been jailed for gross negligence manslaughter in November 2013. I was attending the annual meeting of the Vascular Society when one of my colleagues told me the news. At that time I did not know David Sellu and I knew nothing of the events leading up to the verdict. I was assured by my friend that he was a well-respected and competent colleague. The general feeling among the medical profession was that something had gone very badly wrong at his trial.

I thought nothing further about it until I had a chance meeting with a member of the legal profession while on holiday in Italy during the summer of 2014. We discussed the differences between medical practice in the UK compared with the USA. American surgeons are much more likely to over-investigate and over-treat their patients due to the litigious patients they encounter, who are undoubtedly encouraged by adverts extolling 'no win no fee' legal advice.

After reading the legal documents pertaining to his trial I was shocked to find that, amongst other allegations, David Sellu was made responsible for delays in surgery which were outside his control. It was clear that any surgeon (including myself) could have similar allegations made against them. I decided to help to clear his name. My vascular surgical colleague put me in touch with the Friends of David Sellu, the support group, and I met a remarkable woman called

Jenny Vaughan, a consultant neurologist. Jenny had already investigated the reasons behind David Sellu's conviction and we both agreed that what had happened amounted to a miscarriage of justice. If the verdict was allowed to stand it would alter the behaviour of doctors in the UK, who would start to practise defensive medicine, leading to a huge increase in cost to the health service. Failure to overturn his conviction would also have serious implications for high-risk specialties with regard to recruitment and retention of surgeons. This was a case surgeons, and the country, could not afford to lose.

I have come to admire and respect David Sellu, who with the support of his wife Catherine and their family and friends, has shown remarkable strength of character in dealing with circumstances that could have destroyed a lesser man.

– Professor Peter Taylor, Retired Consultant Vascular Surgeon, Guy's & St Thomas' Hospital and King's College London, MA MB MChir FRCS

Chapter One

'Would the defendant stand up ...'

It took a few seconds to accept who the defendant was. I rose slowly to my feet.

The trial had lasted nearly six weeks. Each morning, as my family and I walked from the tube station to the court, we were mobbed by photographers walking backwards ahead of us with their cameras pointed in our direction. There was an even bigger crowd of paparazzi standing outside the only public entrance into the court and the whirring noise of their cameras was unmistakable. We had been advised to comport ourselves normally, with dignity, and not attempt to hide our faces.

'They will get their pictures anyway, and if not outside the court, it will be on the doorsteps outside your home,' my medicolegal adviser told me.

If I thought events outside were intimidating, I found the interior of the Old Bailey even more daunting, with its wooden panels covering the walls, high ceilings with their ornate linings, the massive corridors, the cavernous court-room. Despite my beta-blocker drug, prescribed to control my high blood pressure, each heartbeat resounded through my chest like a gong.

Sitting low down, across from the judge, I was forced to look up at him on his raised platform. I knew he was in his early sixties from his Wikipedia entry, but he looked older in his wig and glasses. He took all his notes on his laptop and at the beginning of their interrogation, each witness was instructed to speak slowly. The jury were seated on two levels to my left, and between them and the judge was the witness box where I had given evidence for nearly three days. In the well between us sat the prosecuting and defence lawyers and to my right was the public gallery on two floors. I sat in a cage flanked by two prison officers, one of whom was armed with a pair of handcuffs.

A nurse was on stand-by.

The archaic court rituals were well rehearsed. Two loud taps had announced the judge's entrance into the courtroom, which he made through a huge door. He was dressed in garb that would not have looked out of place two centuries ago; we had all stood up and watched him bow to the lawyers, and they in turn bowed back; then we waited for him to sit down, before we did.

I cast a quick glance at my wife and family before facing the judge. I felt frightened and humiliated in equal measure, but tried to show no outward signs of my distress. There were now more people in the courtroom than at any time during the six weeks of the trial. I was aware of the intense medical, legal, press and public interest in my case. It had received unprecedented publicity in the press.

A surgeon on trial for manslaughter.

'David Sellu, for the offence of unlawfully killing Mr James Hughes, I sentence you to two and a half years in prison...'

I could hear low rumblings from all sides of the court and louder voices from the public gallery. The prison warder, who had been standing next to me, took my hand and locked me in handcuffs. As he led me out of the dock, I looked up towards my family, who I could hear crying. I recalled my barrister cross-examining a consultant anaesthetist with whom I had worked closely for nearly twenty years; she had witnessed my work at close quarters.

Defence barrister: 'You said you have known Mr Sellu as a colleague since 1994. You have frequently worked with him in the NHS and in private practice. You have worked with him in the operating theatre?'

Witness: 'Correct.'

Defence barrister: 'Many of these cases were complex and high risk?'

Witness: 'Yes.'

Defence barrister: 'In relation to clinical work in theatre, has that involved Mr Sellu operating on colleagues referred to him?'

Witness: 'Yes.'

Defence barrister: 'Has Mr Sellu been frequently called upon by clinicians in the intensive therapy unit* for his opinion?'

Witness: 'Yes. He is the first port of call for patients with abdominal pain, such is the level of trust of my intensive care colleagues in Mr Sellu.'

Defence barrister: 'How would you describe him as a clinician?'

Witness: 'He is a very good doctor and a very good surgeon. He is meticulous in his planning and diagnostics.

---

* The more modern name for intensive care unit (ICU) is intensive therapy unit (ITU). In colloquial speech, it is easier for people to refer to them both as intensive care.

He is a very caring doctor. I have seen him talk in a sensitive manner to patients with cancer.'

Defence barrister: 'Has he saved lives?'

The answer had been a resounding *Yes*.

+ + +

I do not know my date of birth. Born in Sierra Leone at a time when there were no records of births in my village, I began life in rural Africa where I was destined to find work cultivating rice and looking after a small flock of sheep and goats. I was the first of ten children. My parents never went to school and could neither read nor write English. They were subsistence farmers and even by African standards this was a lowly occupation. They had learned from previous generations that when a piece of land was tilled, it had to lie fallow for five to ten years before the same crop, usually rice, could be grown successfully on it again. When I was older my parents could remember the name of the farm where they worked when I was born and could recall that it was about the start of the harvest season, which was typically November. The best calculations placed my year of birth as between 1948 and 1950.

After many years of infertility, my aunt, who was in her early 40s, had decided that the time had come to look for an opportunity to raise a child born to her sisters' families; she was handed me. My aunt, also illiterate, lived in the provincial capital, Bo, which was where I now found myself. My aunt was a big lady, full of energy. She had learned to be a seamstress and made a living buying materials from Lebanese traders, making dresses and selling them for profit. I would accompany her to neighbours' houses to drop off the dresses and collect payments. Her husband had joined the army during World War II and been recruited to fight with the Allies against the Japanese in Burma.

'The Japanese never took black soldiers as prisoners,' he would say. 'Any black soldiers captured were used for target practice. White soldiers who were captured were kept in prison camps, but were treated badly.'

My uncle fought valiantly and survived and when he returned home at the end of the war, he was given a job as a local tax collector. I suspected that the money he brought home was more than the meagre salary from his job. We lived in a comfortable part of town, had electricity and enough to eat.

My aunt never discussed sending me to school.

Over time, I made friends with the older children who lived a few doors down from us; I would wait for them to get home from school, then go to their house to play. Their parents were primary school teachers and the children always boasted about being at the top of their classes. I dreamed that if I could learn to read and write like them, I too would be a teacher. I did not speak English but entreated them to teach me how to read and write, in return for helping launder their school uniforms and serving as goalkeeper in the street football team. I was good in goal but not much use anywhere else on the pitch.

From then on, I tried to 'read' everything I could lay my hands on, including magazines and newspapers. I began by identifying simple words that I had been shown. I had tried to pronounce unfamiliar words phonetically until my friends cautioned me that many words in English sounded different from the way they were spelled.

'COW as in *cacao*, but MOW as in *Bo*.'

Cacao, I discovered later, was the name we called the plant that produced seeds exported to make chocolate.

They also taught me to write, but again the shapes of the letters and the way in which they were written differed from how the letters and words appeared in books and newspapers. It was not an easy start but I found the challenge fascinating and so I persevered.

I discovered later that my aunt's husband, Solomon, should be referred to as my uncle, not my uncle in law, although I was not related to him by blood. This was just the way it was in English. He was acting as my dad, and I addressed him as *Papa*. His friends called him Solo. He was a tall, well-built man with a moustache and wore his hair parted on one side. He liked to impose discipline, insisting that each day I wake up at 6, help clean the house, fetch water in buckets from a well on the compound and polish his shoes until I could see my reflection in them.

We had electricity but no running water. Every weekend, along with the other local children, I would be sent out into the forest to bring back firewood, which we loaded on our heads, to be used for cooking and boiling water for washing. In return Papa took me fishing and let me ride on the back of his motorbike, which he drove fast. He also bought new clothes for me, but not shoes. I didn't wear shoes before my teens and went everywhere barefoot. Only children from rich families wore shoes.

My friends said I was making good progress with reading and writing. One day one of Papa's friends, a policeman, came to the house and placed the newspaper he was carrying on a table. By now I could read whole sentences, despite not knowing what they meant. I recognised many of the words in the newspaper and read them aloud.

'Solo,' the policeman said to Papa, 'you must get your wife to send this boy to school. Can you not see how well he can read? He can read better than my son who is much older and has been going to school for nearly two years.'

'And I can write too,' I added.

+ + +

I discovered years later that when the headmaster met up with my aunt on my first day at school, between them they determined that my date of birth would be 22 November 1946. What is more accurate is that the headmaster allocated my birth to this date and my aunt agreed. As we did not celebrate birthdays it would be several years before I was to recognise the significance of this date, soon to be inscribed in my passport.

In the evenings my school friends and I would huddle under lamp posts on the streets to do our homework until we were forced by tiredness or mosquitoes to go to bed. Electricity was in short supply and expensive. I gained eight subjects at 'O' level and five at 'A' level, both sets of examinations then conducted by the Cambridge external examinations board. I won a scholarship to study medicine in Manchester after taking a gap year to work as a science teacher in my old school, to earn additional money to subsidise my studies.

In September 1968 I arrived in the UK to start a medical degree. It was my first time on an aeroplane and I was at a loss as to how this machine that weighed so many tonnes could not only take off from the ground, but also fly at high speed and land many thousands of miles away. I was too excited to wonder whether I would get to London safely.

I knew no one in London but I was fortunate to be met by a welcoming group organised by the British Council. I had been on a course organised by the Council from their offices in Freetown, for students travelling to the United Kingdom. They had advised me to look out for their representatives at all the major airports in London.

That evening I was taken with other students to a British Council hostel in Knightsbridge. I was inwardly excited by the different colours of lights on the streets and shops, the amount of traffic and the sheer number of people on the roads. The following morning I discovered to my irritation that I had forgotten my toothbrush, toothpaste and comb in Freetown and I walked to the nearest shop from Hans Crescent, the street on which the hostel was located.

It was a strange shop, the likes of which I had never seen before. It was so big that I had to make a note of where I was each step of the way to make sure I did not get lost. It was called *Harrods*. I walked up to an attendant and explained what I was looking for and that I was new in London. He looked at me sympathetically and said:

'Sir, I would recommend you try a shop called *Boots*. When you go out through that door, turn left; walk past a small road called Hans Road and Boots is on your left, same side as this shop. You can't miss it.'

I did not realise the significance of this shopping faux pas until I recounted this event during freshers' week in university. One freshman shouted out loud:

'Come and listen to this. David Sellu only goes shopping in the most expensive shop in the world.'

It was a source of amusement and some embarrassment when two to three years after I arrived many of my university mates were celebrating their twenty-first birthdays. 'When can we expect to celebrate your twenty-first?' was a frequent question posed to me on these occasions.

'Er...' was the answer I gave many times before I admitted that I celebrated it before I came to university.

+ + +

My two most memorable experiences in England were seeing snow for the first time and watching George Best play for Manchester United.

I gained my degree five years after I began. I trained widely in all aspects of general surgery in major hospitals in Manchester, London, Southampton and Birmingham. I did specialist training in gastrointestinal and colorectal surgery in London and Birmingham. I was awarded the Master of Surgery degree from Manchester University and I hold a Master of Science degree in medical informatics from City University, London. I am a Fellow of the Royal College of Surgeons of both England and of Edinburgh.

+ + +

I met my wife Catherine at Hammersmith Hospital where I trained as a registrar in cardiothoracic surgery and she worked as a staff nurse on the ITU. We married in 1981 and had four wonderful children, Amy, Daniel, Sophie and James.

During the course of our marriage, Catherine and I would return to Sierra Leone to do voluntary work in a mission hospital in Serabu, a small town about thirty miles south of Bo. The Roman Catholic nuns who ran the hospital provided a range of treatments and had a school of nursing that was the envy of government hospitals several times larger. Their results were so impressive that their patients came not only from Sierra Leone but also from surrounding West African countries. The senior doctors and nurses had not taken a holiday in years. One year the senior surgeon welcomed my arrival to go on a long-deserved break. By this time I had been functioning as an experienced surgical registrar in the UK and had done a lot of work independently and successfully and so now, on each occasion I came, I was entrusted to run Serabu Hospital as the sole surgeon. The laboratory and X-ray facilities were very limited but I soon learned to use the scant diagnostic tools to treat a huge variety of conditions and to perform a vast array of operations, with good results.

Once I was asked to see a woman in her forties bleeding from a stomach ulcer. She had vomited so much blood and for so long that by the time she was brought to the hospital she had almost no blood left inside her. She needed a blood transfusion urgently to stand a chance of undergoing an operation to stop the bleeding and save her life. There was no blood in the blood bank. I volunteered to have my blood group checked and fortunately for her it was the same as hers and I was a suitable match to donate for her. I gave her a unit of blood and her condition improved.

I was asked if I could perform her operation, as the only other surgeon was out of the hospital. It was the most meticulous operation I had ever performed. I could not afford to lose any blood, remembering that most of what was inside her was mine and I would not be able to donate any more. To everyone's relief she made an excellent recovery. I described this experience in the widely read *British Medical Journal**

---

* Sellu, D, Personal View, BMJ 1985:290: 1741

when I wrote an article about the differences between the application of technology in western medicine compared to a developing practice.

+ + +

My first consultant post was in Oman in the Middle East, where I worked from 1987 for the Ministry of Health. I also took part in shaping the curriculum of the exciting new medical school and taught undergraduates in the school. Catherine worked as an administrator supervising the programmes of students between the medical school and the prestigious new tertiary hospital, the Royal Hospital.

We stayed in Oman for five and a half years and would have remained there for much longer. The pay was not as generous as in other gulf states such as Saudi Arabia, but we were well looked after and enjoyed being accommodated in a comfortable villa, with a maid to help look after our children as well as earning enough to pay the mortgage for a house we had in Oxfordshire. When Amy, our eldest child, reached the most senior class in her school and there were no higher English schools there, we were faced with the choice of either sending her to boarding school in England (some parents we knew from Britain did that) or returning as a family. Fortunately, I landed a senior job in London at just the right time.

I was now appointed as a full-time senior lecturer in surgery at the Royal Postgraduate Medical School, now Imperial College, and Honorary Consultant Surgeon at Hammersmith Hospital in London. It was while I was at Hammersmith Hospital that I looked after prisoners from HMP Wormwood Scrubs. The two establishments were next to each other and we were the local hospital serving the prison, its staff and inmates. From what I could gather, the attitude of staff to prisoners was to be tough with them:

'Bang 'em up two or three to a cell and make 'em eat, sleep and crap, all in the same place. Make 'em feel this is a prison, not a Butlin's holiday camp. The keyword is deterrence. If they have any sense, they will not want to come back here again.'

From my job in Hammersmith I would go on to work in Ealing Hospital in West London as consultant surgeon with an interest in colorectal surgery. While I was working in Ealing Hospital, I had admitting privileges to the private Clementine Churchill Hospital in Harrow, about seven miles away.*

It never crossed my mind that one day, by a quirk of fate, I would find myself in the situation of discovering first-hand whether the attitudes of doctors towards prisoners had changed.

---

* Ealing Hospital is one of the hospitals closest to Heathrow airport and, on at least three occasions, I looked after people who had been caught by the airport security on suspicion of having ingested drugs. All of these suspects underwent scans and I remember two patients whose scans were highly suggestive. The first of these patients did not have any signs of bowel obstruction or perforation and in such a case it was best to admit the patient for observation. Security guards were present round the clock and they collected all his excrement in special containers. When the patient finally passed the packets of drugs the officer who was present arrested him.

The second patient had bowel obstruction and I operated on him to remove the drugs. This involved opening the bowel near the site where the drug was lodged, removing the package or packages and stitching the bowel back together. The surgical team would spare themselves a great deal of trouble, bureaucracy and legal challenges if they involve an officer throughout the operation: the officer would attend the operation and receive all materials retrieved, as they would need to be analysed and the result used in any subsequent court case.

Chapter Two

11 February 2010, Ealing Hospital, 7.45 a.m. to 6.15 p.m.,
The Clementine Churchill Hospital, 7.00 p.m. to 10.40 p.m.,
then home

Checking my diary, I had an ordinary day ahead. Seven a.m.: I was driving to work on the A40 dual carriageway past Northolt airport, hoping to avoid the heavy traffic coming into London from the direction of Oxford in the west.

Such are the frailties of the human brain that it is difficult to recall events even of yesterday with any degree of accuracy. But I was about to learn that an ability to relate past occurrences with precision could make the difference between a credible defence and a prison sentence in a court of law. As with most working days, I can recall the details of 11 February 2010 only because they were as routine as any other day. My encounters with patients were carefully documented so that I have been able to consult my notes to help me construct what happened on that fateful day.

I had spent the whole of the previous day performing two major cancer operations with a large team of highly dedicated and skilled people, and they had been a success. Technically the operations went smoothly, blood loss was relatively minor and the patients all came through with no immediate complications.

7.45 a.m. The patients were recuperating in the intensive therapy unit (ITU) and I saw them first and then gave their relatives a ring to inform them of progress since we spoke at the end of the previous day.

8.30 a.m. Next it was the Multidisciplinary Cancer Team meeting (MDT). The MDT was an important new forum set up to take the decision about cancer care away from individuals to teams of experts including doctors, nurses and, where possible, lay people. Many had observed that patients, on whose behalf life-and-death decisions were made, were never present in MDTs. This meeting took place in my hospital once a week on a Thursday.

10.00 a.m. The MDT was followed by a busy outpatient clinic that lasted till lunchtime.

12.20 p.m. I fitted in a quick lunch in my office and finished dictating the letters from the clinic for my secretary to pick up and type.

1.10 p.m. I went to the wards to see four ill patients – there was not enough time for a full ward round – and once again I missed the Grand Round held during the lunch break on Thursdays. The Grand Round was an important educational gathering in the postgraduate centre for the whole hospital and the presentation was by a member of a team or a nominated expert outsider to lecture on a topic of interest to a wide audience. My team would take the podium in two weeks and I would definitely be there to support the designated presenter, my specialist registrar: senior input was important for balance and education.

1.30 p.m. Then, an endoscopy list till five, and another visit to the ITU and wards.

6.20 p.m. I packed my bags to go to the Clementine Churchill Hospital, the private hospital in Harrow, about seven miles away, to do an evening clinic booked from seven to nine. It was the evening rush hour and traffic, as would be expected, was particularly heavy in that part of the capital.

My children were by now pursuing their own careers away from home and I expected that my long-suffering wife, alone in the house, would probably be in bed by the time I arrived home. As it turned out, Catherine was still awake when I arrived after 10 p.m. She too had been through a busy day working as matron in charge of a busy Accident and Emergency (A&E) department in the district general hospital, Ealing Hospital, where I practised. She prepared me a late dinner and went to bed as I stayed up to update my records with events of the day, dictate letters to GPs and obtain notes for the following day.

+ + +

Looking back, as I would do over the coming months and years, I would discover that I'd seen two patients in the ITU during the morning and discussed fifteen patients at the MDT. Twenty-one patients consulted me in the clinic at Ealing Hospital up to lunchtime. I visited a further six patients in the ward. In the afternoon I performed endo-scopic examinations on six patients, nearly all of whom I gave intravenous sedation to, as was routine for these tests. Endoscopy involves passing a special camera on the end of a long flexible tube through a body orifice such as the mouth or anus into the hollow body cavity into which it opens. In the case of colonoscopy, for instance, the endoscope is passed through the anus to inspect the inner lining of the large bowel or colon.

At the Clementine Churchill Hospital, the private hospi-tal, I saw on the ward three patients who had been under my care and five in the clinic. About halfway through that clinic I was asked by an orthopaedic consultant colleague, Mr John Hollingdale, to see a patient who was complaining of abdominal pain five days after an elective knee replacement operation.

It was Mr Hughes, my last patient, whom I saw just after 9 p.m., who was to change everything.

Mr Hughes was a sixty-six-year old retired builder. His business had been concentrated in London where some of his family lived, but his main home, which he shared with his wife, was in County Armagh in Northern Ireland. Lying in bed, he was evidently a tall man of stocky build. From the body mass index documented in his nursing notes he had been classified as obese. He stammered slightly as he spoke.

'Hello, Mr Hughes.' I shook his hand gently. 'My name is David Sellu and I am a consultant general and bowel surgeon.' His eyes lit up. 'Your orthopaedic surgeon, Mr Hollingdale, has asked me to come and see you because you have been getting pains in your tummy.'

He seemed relieved. 'Hello, doctor. At last someone I can talk to.'

I pulled up the chair next to his bed and sat down.

'You know, I have been trying to explain to the ward doctor who has been to see me a few times today and to the nurses about my pain, but they do not understand me and I cannot understand what they are saying to me. I had to ring Mr Hollingdale's secretary to ask him to come and see me.'

'I am sorry to hear that,' I responded. 'To save you a lot of repetition, I have looked through your notes and I know it is late in the night. Allow me please to summarise what I know and fill me in on any details I may have missed.'

'OK, doctor.'

'I see you are a retired builder and you flew here from Northern Ireland to have your left knee replacement.'

'My GP's wife, who is also from Northern Ireland, had her knee replaced by Mr Hollingdale and I took his advice to be referred here to this surgeon. She too is a GP and they work together in the same practice. I am a friend of both the GP and his wife.' He was a little breathless as he spoke and had to pause between sentences.

'The knee operation, I see, was five days ago, and aside from some bleeding from the wound, all seems to be going well.'

'That's right. In fact Mr Hollingdale said I could go home in three days but I have asked him if I can stay until my stitches come out. It's been painful to walk but I have managed to walk with the physiotherapist and I have been to the toilet on my own.'

'Tell me about the tummy pain,' I said.

'I woke up at about five o'clock this morning with pain in the lower part of my tummy. I have never had this type of pain before. It got a little worse and then eased for several hours, but it has started again.'

I encouraged Mr Hughes to describe the location and the characteristics of his pain and any aggravating and relieving factors. He said he had drunk a few sips of water during the day, but he was avoiding food, as he felt it might make the pain worse. He had not vomited. I went through the medications he had been taking prior to coming in to hospital and those that were prescribed while he was in. He admitted he drank more alcohol than was good for him but he did not smoke.

I proceeded to do a general examination of Mr Hughes and finished with a gentle but careful check of his tummy. I washed my hands and took leave to go and look at the results of the abdominal and chest X-rays and blood tests he had had earlier that day.

I came back about twenty minutes later:

'I have considered carefully the tummy pain I have come to see you about and I have looked at the tests you had today.' He remained silent as I spoke. 'I suspect you may have a puncture in a part of your bowel. The bowel is a long tube. It's too soon to say if there is a puncture or perforation, or which part of your bowel is affected.'

'Is that serious, doctor?' He sat up as he spoke.

'I don't know at this stage,' I said, as I held his hand gently. 'I will arrange for you to have an intravenous drip because I don't want you to have anything more to eat or drink, to rest your bowel. Also, you are a bit dry and you need fluids to make up the amount you are missing.'

I could sense relief that after a long day, at last something was being done for him.

I continued: 'I will ask the nurses to give you strong pain-killer injections tonight. I will get the resident doctor to do some more tests and I will get him to prescribe some further medicines for you. I will arrange for you to have a CT scan first thing tomorrow.'

I explained what a CT scan was and how it would give us more information to decide what to do next. I told Mr Hughes that CT scans are special pictures obtained using X-rays to create a detailed picture of the body; three-dimensional images that give clearer pictures than an ordinary X-ray. I informed him that some bowel perforations were

more effectively managed by doing a major abdominal operation, but some could be treated in the X-ray department
by the radiologist inserting a tube into the abdominal cavity
with a local anaesthetic under X-ray guidance. We would
know what treatment was appropriate when the CT was
done. For now he agreed with me that his overall general
condition was satisfactory. I informed him that the preliminary tests did not show anything alarming and it was safe to
wait till the morning.

'Where is your wife tonight? Do you want me to ring her
to tell her what I have just told you?' I enquired.

'She is in Northern Ireland. Please don't call her; I don't
want to worry her. In any case, there is nothing she can do
where she is now.' He paused. 'I have a daughter not far
away but I don't want you to bother her either. I will call and
explain what you have just told me.'

'Very well. If there is any more that I can tell them, I'll be
happy to. Good night, Mr Hughes.'

I phoned Mr Hollingdale at the nurses' station to thank
him for the referral and explained my findings and plan of
action. He had inserted a large metal implant in this patient's
knee and any infection on this material would result in cata-
strophic failure of the operation. Antibiotics were important
not only to reduce the chances of implant infection but of
course as part of the management of this abdominal condition. Even though a perforation had not been confirmed, a
proactive administration of antibiotics would be sensible.
Mr Hollingdale agreed and left the choice of antibiotics up
to me. Whether this conversation took place and what was
agreed were debated later, but I stood by my version. I wrote
the word 'Urgent' at the top of the CT scan request form and

handed it to the nurse in charge, explaining that I wanted the test performed first thing in the morning.

I left to go home, a journey of about twenty-five minutes.

Same day, home, about 11 p.m.

I phoned the hospital several times to enquire about anaesthetists, in case I needed to operate on Mr Hughes the next day. The hospital did not have a rota of anaesthetists, something that would be alluded to later in the course of this case. NHS hospitals had anaesthetists on stand-by twenty-four hours a day, but only some private hospitals did. Anaesthetists were difficult to find to put patients to sleep for an emergency and major abdominal operation, a specialised procedure.

I also spoke to the resident hospital doctor, who told me that the tests I had asked him to do were normal. I instructed him to give the patient antibiotics. It transpired later that the doctor in question did not do the tests, even though I had documented the request in the patient's notes and confirmed this with verbal instructions to him. I had been falsely assured that the tests were normal when in fact they had not been carried out. The antibiotics were not prescribed either; that the antibiotics failed to reach the patient would, as it turned out, be blamed on me.

Next day, Friday 12 February 2010, home, about 6.30 a.m.

The nurse who had been looking after Mr Hughes through the night rang me to give me an update. We had always urged nurses to feel free to ring consultants about any matters they wished to report, and so I welcomed the call. The nurse told me that at one point in the night Mr Hughes's urine output, which was being monitored hourly as part of his routine care, had dropped, probably because he was still short of fluid. She had informed the same resident doctor who was looking after him the previous day and he had asked for the intravenous fluid volume to be increased. She did this, and the urine output in subsequent hours had returned to acceptable levels. Overall, she assured me, the patient's condition had otherwise remained stable.

It would later be noted that the same resident doctor had been working for seven days, looking after over a hundred patients, with only short breaks for sleep and refreshment. Such practices, it appears, were common in private hospitals.

Friday 12 February 2010, the Clementine Churchill Hospital, about 9.30 a.m.

I had other patients at the Clementine Churchill Hospital and three pre-booked sessions, one endoscopy list in the morning, another in the early afternoon and a clinic in the evening. I paid a brief visit to Mr Hughes and confirmed that his condition had indeed remained stable save for the problems described earlier by the nurse. (The prosecution would not believe that I made this visit, as I did not write in the notes and the nurse who had been looking after him that morning was busy with other patients in single rooms on the ward.) Mr Hughes had not yet had the CT scan I'd hoped would have been done by 9 a.m., so I rang the imaging department to try to expedite it. This department was occupied with doing elective scans and did not take kindly to interruptions, even for emergency tests. Again, in the course of the enquiries that took place later, I would be held responsible for the delay to the scan.

The Endoscopy Unit, Clementine Churchill Hospital, same day, 10 a.m.

I performed one endoscopy test for which I gave the sedative myself. I finished at 10.45 a.m. and went to see three other patients on other wards in the hospital. The CT scan on Mr Hughes had still not been done.

I drove home to collect some records I needed that afternoon and came back to do another endoscopy that had been booked that afternoon. On my way back I received a phone call to inform me that Mr Hughes had had his CT scan and it showed a perforation of his large bowel. From the description given, it was clear the only way to deal with this was to perform a major operation to remove the perforated section of his bowel. Such perforations cannot be repaired by stitching them up, because the large bowel surrounding the hole is diseased and will not hold stitches.

Car Park, Clementine Churchill Hospital, same day, 1.47 p.m.

I rang the theatre to find out when there would be a free slot available to perform an emergency operation on Mr Hughes. The definition of *emergency* is often confused and the jury grappled with this issue during my trial. In a medical setting it is the opposite of *elective* – in other words, it's unplanned, but that alone does not define the speed with which action needs to be taken. Emergency operations can be performed within twenty-four to forty-eight hours, depending on the condition of the patient. (Elective operations are scheduled days, weeks and months ahead, whereas emergency operations, by their very nature, are not.) Mr Hughes's condition did not require an *immediate* operation. However, if a free theatre was available and I had an anaesthetist, I would have cancelled all my other engagements that day and proceeded to operate on Mr Hughes.

I know the time of the phone call because it would be included on my mobile phone records, which were to form an important part of the documents used by the prosecution. From my experience such an operation would take at least four hours (including the time to put the patient to sleep and wake them up) and the patient would require a general anaesthetic (GA). Given that Mr Hughes had had a major operation only six days earlier I wanted an experienced anaesthetist who specialised in such operations.

The nurse I spoke to told me the next available slot without invoking a breakthrough procedure would be about 7 p.m. A breakthrough procedure is the act of interrupting an operating list in progress in order to carry out a more urgent procedure. I did not invoke a breakthrough procedure, as I did not have an anaesthetist – it would be reckless for a surgeon to interrupt another's session and then admit that there is no anaesthetist.

The next task was to look for an anaesthetist. By chance, that afternoon at 2 p.m. I was performing another endoscopy examination on a patient who had requested to be fully anaesthetised and not merely sedated. Sedated patients are aware and often communicate with those around them, but their appreciation of pain is reduced. Anaesthetised patients are fully asleep and are rendered pain free. I had booked an anaesthetist for this patient but this anaesthetist was not going to be available to help me operate on Mr Hughes because she had other engagements later that day and in any case there was no theatre yet available. She did, however, kindly help me find an anaesthetist who was going to be in the Clementine Churchill Hospital at 6 p.m. that day to anaesthetise for what was described as a short gynaecological procedure expected to last about an hour. This meant that by about 7 p.m. that day, I would have a free theatre and an anaesthetist. It had taken a considerable amount of time and numerous phone calls by my anaesthetist and me to find someone willing to assist.

I was frequently asked during subsequent investigations why I had not transferred Mr Hughes to an NHS hospital, where, it was assumed, the operation would be done much more quickly. In my many years of practice, I had referred patients in similar circumstances within the NHS, and also received patients from other hospitals. If such a referral was to be considered, the 'referrer' had to find a hospital that had a surgeon free to operate, an intensive care unit with facilities to receive the patient after such a major operation and a free bed to transfer the patient to once they no longer needed ITU facilities. Simply putting a patient in an ambulance and sending them to the nearest hospital would be irresponsible and dangerous, for if the facilities described above were not all available, the patient would end up being transferred to yet another hospital, sometimes a considerable distance away. Multiple journeys in an ambulance are risky and impact negatively on the chances of survival.

The hospital receiving a patient following a transfer has to prioritise the patient among already existing sick patients in the receiving hospital. It is not unknown for the patient to be operated on twenty-four or more hours after arrival in the new location. We already had an ITU bed for Mr Hughes in the Clementine Churchill Hospital and so it was a matter of waiting hopefully until a theatre was empty.

On my way from the car park to the hospital I met the radiologist who had performed and reported the scans and he confirmed that Mr Hughes indeed had a perforation of his large bowel; he had sent a detailed report to the ward.

The endoscopy I was doing at 2 p.m. was delayed while we looked for an anaesthetist but as soon as I finished I went to see Mr Hughes on the ward to update him about events.

Blenheim Suite, Clementine Churchill Hospital, same day, 4 p.m.

Mr Hughes's CT scan report was pinned on the front of his notes and I had a careful look at it before I saw him in his room. He was still in pain but had been receiving intravenous injections of the powerful painkiller morphine, with reasonable effect. He said he was unwell but overall, his condition remained stable.

'The CT scan you had this morning,' I explained, again sitting on a chair next to his bed, 'shows that your large bowel has ruptured or become perforated. The perforation is due to a condition called diverticular disease.' I said this slowly to make sure that he understood everything I was telling him, and he was listening attentively.

I continued: 'Diverticular disease is a condition that affects our large bowels as we grow older and it causes areas of weakening of the wall of the large bowel.'

I drew a diagram to show that in the parts of the bowel affected, the muscle in the bowel wall had mysteriously thinned or completely disappeared, meaning the integrity of the bowel at that point was provided by just the inner and outer linings of the bowel, with no supporting muscle. 'This increases the potential for that part of the bowel to rupture when the pressure inside the bowel increases, as the bowel contracts to expel stools inside it. The rupture can happen at any time in later life; I do not believe the operation you went through six days ago had anything to do with this perforation.' (I first saw Mr Hughes five days after he had his knee operation but I performed his bowel operation six days after that original surgery.)

'I understand what you are saying, doctor,' Mr Hughes said, with a look of relief on his face, but keen not to interrupt, as he knew I had more to say.

'The contents of the large bowel, which are stools or faecal matter, spill into the bowel cavity and that is why you got the tummy pain. But that's not all; the stools contain a lot of bacteria and these cause infection in your tummy cavity. The infection can spread to your bloodstream.'

Mr Hughes shut his eyes momentarily and opened them and continued to look at me. I went on: 'An operation on your tummy is the only option we have now. We have been phoning around today and I have managed to get an anaesthetist who will put you to sleep completely, so you do not feel the operation.'

I stopped for a moment to make sure the nurse who was with me in the room was also listening.

'I am going to do a major operation in which I will make a large cut to open your tummy and remove the affected part of the bowel and clean out the infection.' He nodded. 'When we cut away a portion of bowel, we are left with two ends.' I rolled my fingers with the index finger and thumb of each hand to show the open bowels. 'If there is no infection, we join the ends of the bowels together with stitches or staples or both.' I brought my hands together so that the thumb and index finger of each hand touched the corresponding digit on the other hand. 'But when there is infection, as in your case, the bowel will not take well to having stitches and you could suffer another perforation.'

I referred again to the piece of paper I had been drawing on and drew another diagram of the tummy and the bowel. 'In your case, I will close the lower piece of bowel and leave it inside and bring the upper piece of bowel through the tummy wall as a colostomy.'

I was about to go on to explain what a colostomy was but he nodded and said: 'Oh, yes; I know of people who have colostomy and they wear bags to collect their poo.'

'That's correct,' I replied. 'In your case, the bag will be temporary, and once you have recovered from the operation I will operate to reverse it for you so you can use your normal passage again to pass stools.'

'As you say, doctor, I have no choice,' Mr Hughes said in response. 'I am keen to get rid of this pain and to get better.' He paused and asked: 'Was any of this my fault, did I bring this on myself?'

I held his hand and reassured him he had done nothing wrong and it was the luck of the draw. 'I will get a specialist nurse to come and see you after the operation to give you advice on how to manage your bag.'

'A stoma nurse,' he added.

'That is correct,' as I nodded.

I went on to explain the benefits of the operation and the potential complications, which included infections, deep vein thrombosis or blood clots in the legs and bleeding. It was a legal requirement that the patient gave informed consent, but Mr Hughes made it clear I did not need to go into too much detail and he was willing to sign his consent form, so we could begin to get ready for the operation.

Consulting Rooms, Clementine Churchill Hospital,
same day, 5–7 p.m. and after

Before arriving at the consulting rooms, I rang the anaesthetist who was going to anaesthetise Mr Hughes to give him background information about the patient and to discuss the operation I was proposing to do. He confirmed the information I had been given that he would be in the hospital at 6 p.m. and would call for the patient to be taken to theatre as soon as the other operation he was involved in was over.

I proceeded to the consulting rooms and saw four or five patients. In between these patients I phoned Blenheim Suite to enquire about Mr Hughes and I was reassured that his condition remained unchanged.

Just after 7 p.m., I walked to theatre, which was in the opposite part of the building but on the same floor. I asked the nurse in charge when we could send for Mr Hughes, and this was the first time I was informed there was a problem. The gynaecologist needed the help of another consultant, which meant that there would be a delay, but the anaesthetist was unable to come and talk to me about it. I went back to the consulting rooms and returned forty-five minutes later.

This time I insisted on talking to the anaesthetist who had agreed to operate with me.

He came out and explained that the matter was out of his hands but he would send for Mr Hughes as soon as the operation he was involved in was over. I had no choice in the matter. I did try to phone other anaesthetists but as was to be expected on a Friday evening, no one was available.

Theatre, Clementine Churchill Hospital, same day,
10 p.m. to 4 a.m. the following day

Mr Hughes came to the theatre nearly three hours after his operation had been scheduled. While I was waiting for him I logged into the hospital computer system via a terminal inside the theatre, to go over the results of the CT scans and also for the first time to look at the pictures. Viewing the pictures helped me plan locations to explore during the operation but was not necessary for determining whether an operation was required. That decision had been made from the verbal and written reports I had received from the radiologist.

Mr Hughes was anaesthetised and placed on the operating table. I had scrubbed, put on my theatre gown and cleaned the abdomen with antiseptic. I isolated the operation area with sterile drapes (all materials at or near the operation site are sterilised beforehand) and was about to start cutting the tummy open when the anaesthetist asked me to stop. The patient's condition had suddenly deteriorated; his blood pressure had dropped and his pulse rate had risen, both significantly. This was dangerous. He called the senior anaesthetist on call for the ITU, referred to as an *intensivist*, who was more experienced in dealing with such problems. The intensivist arrived quickly, helped to improve the patient's condition and gave the go-ahead for me to start the operation.

1 a.m.

This was already a difficult operation: I encountered more bleeding than I had expected. There were a number of possible explanations for the bleeding, including infection around the bowels now spreading into the blood; this impairs the ability of the blood to clot normally. I noted also that Mr Hughes had cirrhosis of his liver. Cirrhosis is a condition in which the liver is damaged and its cells are replaced by scar tissue. This causes a knobbly appearance on the surface of the liver that is easy to diagnose. Cirrhosis was another cause of the patient's bleeding. The liver is responsible for manufacturing the proteins that help blood to clot following injury and during operations. Cirrhosis impairs the production of these proteins. Moreover, it is well recognised that patients with cirrhosis have a higher chance of death following major operations than those without cirrhosis. The liver plays an important part in recovery from operations.

My part of the operation took three hours, after which Mr Hughes was sent to the ITU. In all he had been in theatre for nearly six hours. The intensivist told me that he had been in constant contact with Mr Hughes's wife during the operation and told her he was critically ill. She was going to make her way to the hospital from Northern Ireland.

I pondered over the day as I drove home. This had been an exhausting day for all concerned but by no means unusual for me. I had stayed up many times to operate on seriously ill patients.

Mr Hughes's condition was serious. Over a third of people who had perforated diverticular disease died from it, even in the best hospitals in the world. The two other factors in play were the fact that he had not fully recovered from a major knee operation and the presence of cirrhosis of his liver. We had removed his diseased and perforated large bowel but, as I would find out in the morning, he was now fighting for his life because of the consequences of his illness. The significant bleeding I encountered and his liver cirrhosis had seriously tipped the scales against him.

Ealing Hospital, Saturday 13 February 2010, 11 a.m.

I arrived at Ealing Hospital at about 11 a.m. I was keen to ensure that all patients under my care were fully cared for. I went to the ITU where I saw my two patients and then to the wards where I saw about eight patients. Then I set off for the Clementine Churchill Hospital.

ITU, Clementine Churchill Hospital, Saturday 13 February, 2010, 2 p.m.

In the ITU the anaesthetists kept Mr Hughes unconscious and a machine was breathing for him through a tube inserted into his airway. Medications were given to support his heart and kidneys, which were failing. He had come off the operating table just over nine hours ago and it was still early to predict his chances of recovery, but they were not good. I enquired about his family and the senior nurse looking after him said to me:

'The ITU consultant, registrar and I have had a long chat with his wife and some of his children. They are in the visitors' room and as you can imagine they are very upset. We described what happened to him in graphic detail and I do not think they want to hear any more. We thought it was best to leave them alone for now.'

As there was nothing more I could contribute to his care, I left him in the hands of the ITU staff. There was a directory with the phone numbers of all doctors working in the hospital by all phones in the hospital, including in the ITU, but I wrote my mobile number on the front of Mr Hughes's charts as well.

Ealing Hospital, Sunday 14 February 2010, about 4 p.m.

At Ealing Hospital at 11 a.m., I saw the patients I had in the ITU and on the wards. Sunday was the day when, even though I was not on duty, I almost always went in to do the large pile of paperwork that had remained unattended during the week. There were about thirty referral letters from GPs asking me to see patients with a huge variety of problems. Any patient a GP saw who they wanted seen on the same day was either referred to the Accident and Emergency department or discussed with me on the phone. I needed to prioritise those for whom I received letters into three broad categories: those to be seen in two weeks in the clinics; those who could wait six weeks; and those whose problems did not warrant action till later (the time limit was unspecified). Of course if there had been no constraints on resources, everyone would have been given an appointment to be seen within a week or two. I received three times more referrals each week than I had room to accommodate. I had to ration, regrettably.

My mobile phone rang at about 4 p.m. It was the consultant in charge of the ITU who had been called in to assist with Mr Hughes's care:

'Hi David, this is Gary. I'm afraid I have bad news.' He sounded tired and upset and I guessed what he was going to say next: 'Mr Hughes died at 15.38. I have spoken to the relatives and I will issue a death certificate.' Gary went on to explain that not surprisingly they had taken the news badly. Everyone had done their best.

That last statement is one every healthcare worker mulls over after the death of a patient. *Was the death inevitable? Is there more we could have done or could we have handled this case differently?*

Thus began a series of investigations that was to last nearly eight years.

Chapter Three

The internal investigation at the Clementine Churchill Hospital was conducted by the now defunct company, Healthcare Performance Ltd. The investigators were Dr Mike Roddis, who had a background in pathology, and Mr James Eccersley, a consultant colorectal surgeon of Burton Hospitals. They were asked by Professor Duncan Empey, Group Medical Director of the parent company running the hospital, BMI, to look into not only the case of Mr Hughes but to do a full trawl through all my work over the previous years to see where I might have made mistakes, to look for the so-called smoking gun.

The first point to make here is: put any surgeon's work under such close scrutiny and they will have cases that went badly – we are all human and we do not always make perfect decisions. (I suspect even those doing the investigation did not always work in blameless environments – between 2003 and 2006 a worrying 15.6 per cent of patients, or one in six, undergoing large bowel cancer surgery at Burton Hospital NHS Foundation Trust allegedly died within thirty days of their operation, the highest mortality in the country, bbc.com/news/health-13038070, 12 April 2011.)

Second, if I had mismanaged patients, the matter should have been dealt with then and there, and not many years later.

It's worth noting that my management of the three extra cases chosen had not previously been flagged up by the hospital as a cause for concern. Healthcare Performance dropped one of these cases but took me to task in the management of the other two. Every individual patient matters, but after nearly fifteen years of practice, over three thousand patients and many thousands of patient encounters and scores of major and complex operations, this is not a bad result.

Third, the role of the hospital and any failings in its systems were unknown at this stage. As we came to find out later, these findings were suppressed throughout my subsequent case.

Fourth, the training and qualification of the investigators to carry out such an enquiry and their impartiality were unknown and were never questioned.

+ + +

Healthcare Performance issued a critical report, referred to unofficially as the Empey report, into my handling of the index case but suppressed the Root Cause Analysis (RCA) carried out by the hospital's own quality manager, Pam Phull. The RCA was frank and hard-hitting in its criticism of many of the hospital's procedures and personnel, including the nurses and the intensive therapy unit (ITU) outreach team, but this document only came to light after my incarceration, following Subject Access requests and from an investigation by the *Mail on Sunday* (reported on 26 July 2015). It was not produced at the inquest (in contravention of a statutory requirement) and was not alluded to at my trial. It showed that the hospital had major failings that in the view of the manager amounted to substandard management. She proposed a number of remedies. Another failing was the lack of an emergency anaesthetic rota, something I argued was a necessity without which a hospital could not be deemed compliant in its duty to implement an effective breakthrough procedure.

Moreover, this patient's condition was satisfactory and had remained stable and did not justify the immediate operation required, say, in the case of patients with life-threatening bleeding.

It is misleading and unfair to judge the actions of a clinician without taking account of the environment in which they worked and the prevailing practice at the time. Unfortunately, this was not restricted to clinical assessors; as we shall see later, the prosecutors and the experts for the prosecution in my trial, who had had no training in how to give expert testimony, were prepared to overlook systemic failings.

I continued to work at the Clementine Churchill Hospital until September 2010 when my practising privileges were suspended, a month before the inquest into Mr Hughes's death. I was also reported by the hospital to the GMC who summoned me to appear at a hearing in their London office three days before the inquest.

The General Medical Council hearing
(the first of about twelve in my case)

There are a number of organisations that a doctor needs to belong to in order to enable them to practise and/or to help them progress with their education and skills. All doctors have to be registered with the GMC, which determines whether they are fit to practise. The British Medical Association is their trade union and like other such unions, it looks after their rights in the workplace, negotiates their contracts and salaries and helps with their further education.

The Royal Colleges set standards that doctors progressing further in their careers have to meet and the examinations they have to pass to become specialists. To become a specialist in surgery, for example, a doctor has to pass the examination of a Royal College, of which there are a number in Great Britain and Ireland. On passing the examination the title of Member or Fellow is conferred on the doctor.

Another set of bodies such as the Medical Protection Society (MPS) and the Medical Defence Union (MDU) look after doctors' interests if they get into legal difficulties or are the subject of an enquiry, for example after a medical error or a patient's death. Doctors working in NHS hospitals are covered by crown indemnity, but it was a requirement for those working in private practice to take out extra protection. The premium depends on the specialty and the amount earned from such work, after reasonable expenses had been deducted. Those in high-risk disciplines such as obstetrics, orthopaedics, general surgery (including colorectal surgery) and cosmetic surgery could expect to pay more than those in areas of specialism considered to be lower risk. There were other indemnity bodies. Most doctors belong to several of these organisations and have to pay annual fees to each in order to retain their membership.

Before June 2012, panels set up by the GMC heard all allegations of medical misconduct. In each case a GMC barrister formulated the charges and presented them to a team composed of GMC-appointed members. Panels, typically comprising three people, were made up of a doctor and a lay member and were supported by a legal assessor, who instructed them on matters relating to law. The doctor under investigation was invited to bring their own barrister and the proceedings were adversarial, as in a typical court case. The panels, having heard the evidence from both sides, gave judgment and where appropriate the sanctions it considered necessary 'to protect the public and to uphold the reputation of the profession'. These sanctions took many forms, depending on the gravity of the misdemeanour. The GMC could issue a warning, restrict the doctor's practice, suspend them temporarily or remove them entirely from the register. In some cases, the charges were dismissed and no sanctions were imposed. Many criticised the GMC for acting as prosecutor, judge, jury and executioner, all rolled into one. There were also complaints that doctors from ethnic minorities were disproportionately investigated compared to those who were white. Moreover, the scrutiny of GMC investigations took a serious toll on doctors: in 2003/4, between 4 and 5 per cent, or sixty-eight of those doctors being investigated, died, many by taking their own lives. Their median age was forty-five.

In response to some of these criticisms, the GMC set up a new body, the Medical Practitioners Tribunal Service (MPTS) in June 2012, to take over the function of hearing the allegations, judging them and issuing the penalties as appropriate. The GMC retained the role of prosecutor. Observers wondered about the independence and partiality of the MPTS, given that it was paid for by the GMC and it reported to the GMC (as well as Parliament).

October 2010

I was summoned to appear in the GMC London office at Regent's Place on the Euston Road. Mine was one of the last hearings to be held in London before they moved their offices to Manchester (to save on the high rental costs in the capital, I was told).

By way of preparation the MPS had arranged for me to see a barrister specialising in medical negligence and with experience of defending doctors at the GMC and in coroners' courts. She was a young woman in a central London practice and Catherine accompanied me to see her in her chambers a week or so before the hearing. Two medicolegal advisors from the MPS were also in attendance. The barrister had been sent my files in advance and she recited the case accurately. She asked me a number of questions about my background and about the case and when the meeting was over, Catherine and I departed, leaving the rest of the group to continue deliberations. It was always unnerving for me, not knowing what further discussions took place about me at the end of gatherings such as this.

On the day of the hearing Catherine and I took the underground to Euston Square in London, a short walk to the GMC. The offices were in a building on the main thoroughfare running from West London past Euston station. The outside wall facing the main road was glass from floor to ceiling and in the window was a huge statue of a naked man with his back to the public. We went through the security gates and took a lift to the second floor occupied by the GMC. We registered, were given name badges and were shown into a cold room where we were joined by the barrister a short time later. A medicolegal advisor from the MPS arrived almost immediately.

My case was listed for the middle of the morning, but we were finally summoned into a large hall wired with microphones sometime after lunch. My barrister and I were allocated the seats immediately by the door and the prose-cuting team were opposite us. To the far left, between these two rows of seats, were the panel with their names on the table in front of their chairs. The hearings were not open to the public, so my barrister asked permission for my wife to be present. This was granted.

She sat at the opposite end of the room facing the panel.

The chair introduced herself and everybody else on her panel, including the clerk. I was asked to say my name and my GMC registration number.

'David Sellu, 1623518,' I said, as clearly as I could.

These, I would later realise, were the only words I would be allowed to say throughout the session.

The prosecuting barrister for the GMC read out the charges, which I recognised as having been taken almost verbatim from the Empey report. (He did not then read the patient's case notes to get more accurate and first-hand information of the events that led to this patient's death.) He closed his case by saying: 'We conclude by declaring that Mr Sellu's treatment of patient JH fell below the standard expected of a consultant colorectal surgeon to a serious degree, particularly in regard to his operative care.'

I was in shock.

I had never been criticised as a doctor: over the course of my career, I had always been praised as a caring surgeon, a skilled operator and a good teacher by those with whom I had worked. I had kept up to date with all the advances in my field. Even the Empey report had not criticised my operative care; on the contrary, the way I performed the patient's operation had been declared faultless. Most of all, my patients had frequently written to show their appreciation for my care and compassion. The panel asked a number of questions seeking clarification on some of the points the barrister had made, and then it was my barrister's turn.

She spoke clearly and eloquently and all her facts were accurate. The document from which I am quoting is a long one but I give below excerpts of her submission:

'... I therefore wish to begin with a little background to tell you about Mr Sellu before coming on to deal with matters that arise from the report.

'Mr Sellu first qualified in medicine in 1973 from the University of Manchester and he trained as a surgeon in Manchester, London and Birmingham. He obtained his Fellowship of the Royal of Surgeons in 1978 and was appointed a consultant surgeon in 1987. He took up his position as a Consultant General Surgeon specialising in colorectal surgery at the Ealing Hospital in 1993. He began working as a consultant in private practice at the Clementine Churchill Hospital in 1997, some thirteen years ago.

'The report that has been commissioned by (ultimately) BMI Healthcare Ltd was a report that Mr Sellu understands was prompted by a review of all of the cases that he had dealt with throughout his time at the Clementine Churchill Hospital. Over the last thirteen years Mr Sellu has seen in the region of 4,500 patients in private practice at the Clementine Churchill Hospital. He has had in the region of 20,000 patient encounters. One third or 300 to 400 of those patients are patients who have had complex surgery of the like seen in the case of Mr H. That, of course, does not take into account Mr Sellu's NHS practice. You will no doubt be aware from what you have read and what you have heard that there were no previous concerns or complaints made about Mr Sellu's private practice until this report was produced. Similarly when considering his NHS practice, it is important for the panel to know that no complaints or concerns have been raised at all in relation to his NHS practice. Mr Sellu is just as busy in his NHS practice and since ... That, I hope, puts in context the matters that are before you today.

'In essence, the criticisms or concerns that have been raised in the case of Patient H are those of a delay essentially in getting this patient to theatre. It is clear, I hope, to those reading that Mr Sellu recognised in this patient a perforation and that he began taking steps following his first contact with that patient to arrange appropriate treatment and appropriate investigations. It has been highlighted within the body of the report that antibiotics as a matter of fact were not given to this patient. It is also clear from the report that Mr Sellu instructed the RMO at the hospital to initiate antibiotic therapy.' (The RMO was the Resident Medical Officer.)

The barrister spoke for nearly an hour uninterrupted. She highlighted my unblemished forty-year career in medicine and read from testimonies from some of my colleagues who gave excellent references. The panel were told I had never been in front of the GMC, had saved many lives, was a good teacher and was always on hand to manage difficult cases in the intensive care unit and elsewhere. She gave a full background to the case and explained how none of my actions could be judged against prevailing practice as being below standard. Questions from the panel followed. This was when the panel needed to deliberate and to get their decisions typed up.

We left the room and returned to the hall, doing our best to avoid discussing the case; perhaps understandably, the barrister did not want to guess the outcome.

We returned about an hour and a half later for the verdict.

The panel declared that, having heard all the evidence and weighed it up carefully, they had come to the conclusion that I had 'no case to answer' and 'no conditions' would be placed on my practice. They were aware that there was an inquest the following week and would review this decision in light of the outcome.

I thanked my barrister. On the way home, we stopped for a drink in one of the Euston Road pubs. It was not over yet, but we had surmounted one very big hurdle.

+ + +

I was referred to my NHS hospital where a copy of the Empey report by Healthcare Performance was sent. The Trust Board at my hospital considered the report but saw no reason to suspend me from my NHS work, which I continued to do. This report had now been used twice against me, once at the GMC and again at Ealing Hospital, but so far did not have the effect the authors had explicitly desired.

Chapter Four

18 October 2010

Those who believe that hospitals are intimidating have not experienced a coroner's inquest, and certainly not when their work is under microscopic scrutiny. I have frequently advised fellow surgeons to do all they can to fight their case in the operating theatre, clinics and wards and do everything they can to avoid an inquest or litigation. An inquest is held in a court of law: all evidence given is on oath and any falsehood is a criminal offence.

I had read over the case well enough but not in the detail required for taking the stand. I was due to give evidence on the third day according to the schedule released by the coroner's office; my plan was to spend the first day familiarising myself with procedures.

I had taken all of that week off and was planning to use the next two days to prepare my case.

Catherine and I drove to Barnet, North London, to locate the coroner's court the day before the inquest. While there we also looked for suitable parking nearby. We wanted to avoid delays and minimise the possibility of anything going wrong. I was feeling anxious.

Our son Daniel had come from Muscat the week before to comfort us through this unfamiliar process. I had last been inside a coroner's court in the late 1970s in the north of England following the death of a patient with inflammation of the pancreas (pancreatitis) resulting from a severe road traffic accident. The evidence I gave then was brief and after a short hearing the coroner passed a verdict of accidental death. That was easy.

This morning, as I drove to the inquest into Mr Hughes's death, I was filled with foreboding. Yet I was convinced that this unfortunate patient had died from blood poisoning from perforation of his bowel, caused by a natural condition, diverticular disease, and from what I saw when I operated, there was nothing I could have done to save his life.

We arrived about an hour before the start of the inquest and parked in an already crowded car park. We had decided to forgo coffee in the nearby coffee shop and instead headed straight for the court. Many of the staff from the Clementine Churchill Hospital who had been involved in the patient's care were beginning to arrive. The hospital had arranged a minibus to bring their nurses and technical staff. These meetings were open to the public too and I saw a group of people, some of whom I believed I had seen in the hospital during the deceased's illness.

I met my barrister in her wig and robe and she ushered me into the courtroom. She was the same barrister who had represented me at the GMC hearing the previous week. She showed me where to sit in the row immediately behind her. I presumed it was so that if she wanted to ask me any question during the proceedings I was not far away. There were other people dressed in legal robes; some I would discover were acting for the family and others for the hospital. This was the moment when I realised that this enquiry was much more serious than I had imagined. This coroner was one of the few in the country, I was told, who insisted on full legal attire for the barristers during inquests.

There were other doctors in my row, but the family were seated in a separate area at the far end. At the front of the court was a high table with a regal-looking chair facing the court and to the right the witness stand, with books on the ledge. Behind me were people dressed in suits with laptops, some with pictures on their screens of the court building. These were reporters, I surmised, and I was right. I estimated there were over five hundred people in the court that morning.

When the coroner arrived, we all stood up. We sat down when he did. He was a small man with a fierce reputation and came straight to the point:

'The purpose of this court is to establish four things: who this man was, where he died, when he died and how he died.' He looked around and concluded: 'No one is on trial here.'

The family were the first on the stand and the purpose of their statements was to describe the deceased's life and his relationship with his family. He was described as a warm, loving and hard-working man to whom his family meant a great deal. The first medical witness was the Bulgarian doctor who was the RMO in the hospital. He was on duty when Mr Hughes was in the hospital and had been called to see him several times during the course of the day when the patient complained of abdominal pain. He prescribed painkillers and a bowel relaxant but admitted he did nothing more active for the patient. He called Mr John Hollingdale, the patient's consultant orthopaedic surgeon, in the early evening and requested blood tests and abdominal and chest X-rays on Mr Hollingdale's instructions. The RMO was questioned until we broke up for lunch.

After lunch the coroner decided that he had changed his mind about the order of proceedings: I was required to give my evidence next.

I was not prepared for this. I had not expected to be on the stand till day three. My barrister turned around and told me to give it my best. I came out in a cold sweat and my heart pounded. Shaking off a feeling of paralysis, I now had to get up when called and muster the energy to face the inquest.

I took the stand, where I was sworn in. Then commenced a series of quick-fire questions to which I hardly had time to give answers. The coroner banged his right index finger several times on the table as he spoke and raised his voice at my answers. It was clear from his body language that I was in for a difficult session.

When did I qualify; what was my area of specialism in surgery; what was I doing on the evening of 11 February 2010; what was my experience of treating people with emergency abdominal problems? Questions then turned to my involvement in Mr Hughes's care up to the end of the operation the following day. The coroner frequently interrupted me to ask questions before I had time to finish answering the previous one.

The following exchange took place, extracted from the transcripts of the inquest.

Coroner: 'So just so that I understand it, at about 2, when you saw the results of the CT scan, you were made aware of a collection of material in the abdomen, with it likely having come from a perforation. Was not that at that point an emergency? Once you had evidence that there was contamination within the abdomen?'

Answer from me: 'Yes, and I began to take steps to ensure that... I had already started taking steps, even from the evening before, to look for anaesthetists.' It was obvious I was nervous. This was several questions rolled into one.

The coroner did not make it clear what he meant by the *results* of the CT scan. The radiologist had written a comprehensive report on the scans and he communicated it to me when I encountered him at lunchtime. I saw this report when I went to review the patient at about 4 p.m. that afternoon.

Results of CT scans and the pictures were also stored in the hospital-wide computer system. I had viewed these just before I carried out the patient's operation later that night.

The difference between my seeing the printed results of the scans in the afternoon and my viewing of the pictures at night was to form an important aspect of the case against me.

The next stage of the inquest was my interrogation by the barrister for the family. I do not recall how long this lasted but in the course of it, the coroner said to the barrister:

'I am going to interrupt you.'

He went on, addressing me: 'I am going to ask you to step outside court for a moment and I am going to ask my Coroner's Officer M... to take you downstairs so you can have somewhere to sit rather than up here, because there is a matter that I need to discuss with counsel. Would you be so kind as to step outside the court?'

+ + +

I found myself ushered out of the court downstairs to the narrow entrance hall where there was a long wooden bench. It was as if I'd told a patient who was suffering from cancer, whom I was about to operate on, to leave the consulting room so I could relay his diagnosis and treatment to his family and to the people in the waiting room.

Wasn't I entitled to the information he was giving the court?

The next forty minutes seemed like a lifetime.

I was surprised when people I had seen in the courtroom now began to walk past me to the front door. They walked as close to the far wall as possible, as if trying to avoid me, turning to steal a brief look in my direction but avoiding making eye contact. I did not know what had happened nor what had been said in the courtroom.

A senior manager from the Clementine Churchill Hospital walked past me with a mobile phone. I greeted her, 'Hello...', but she ignored me.

It appeared that the rest of the world was about to be told the result of the day's deliberation, something that was denied to me.

What the hell is going on? I said to myself.

+ + +

It was some time before my barrister came out, now walking towards me with my family in tow. While the barrister appeared composed, Catherine and Daniel were wearing telltale expressions of dejection that told me the news was not good.

'Hang on, Mr Sellu,' the barrister said as she walked past me and had a brief chat with the lawyers representing the family and the hospital.

'Not very good news, Dad,' Daniel said quickly, confirming my fear.

Catherine looked too shaken to even say a word. My barrister came back to me and asked me to follow her into a small room off the corridor. I was trying to digest what Daniel had just told me and anxious to be filled in on the details.

'I am afraid the inquest has been adjourned,' the barrister said, presumably pausing to get a reaction. I tried not to betray one. 'The coroner is going to refer this case to the police as he suspects a crime has been committed.'

'What crime, and by whom?' I said, stunned.

My mind went into overdrive. Was it the hospital? My mind flashed back to the lack of an anaesthetic rota in the hospital and my inability to operate when the elective procedure being performed that evening overran. Employing a single doctor to cover a busy hospital with over a hundred patients and making him work seven days in a stretch? Was it the RMO? He had been called numerous times to see the patient and it had taken him a long time to summon the patient's consultant. Was it the nurses? I had become aware of the patient's frustration to get the nurses and the RMO to understand his concerns and in desperation he had phoned his consultant's secretary. Was it the anaesthetist, who had seen the patient and yet scheduled an elective operation before what was an emergency procedure for my patient?

Hang on. Was it *me*?

Only two doctors had given evidence so far, the RMO and I. The RMO was allowed to finish giving his evidence, but I had been interrupted and now the inquest had been adjourned. Surely not?

'The allegation is manslaughter, against you,' she said after that brief pause.

'Surely I did not kill Mr Hughes,' I protested.

'I am afraid that is the law. The coroner is entitled to adjourn the inquest if he suspects a crime has been committed. You have not been charged,' she paused, '*yet.*'

'You mean neither the RMO nor the hospital is being charged, after what we've just heard?' Daniel demanded.

This was a sensible question, and one that had crossed my mind. I was looking forward to a time when someone in higher authority would force the hospital to correct some of the inadequacies uncovered by this inquest.

'Not necessarily, but that is up to the police.' The barrister stood up, looked at me and then my wife and son and concluded: 'I will send a report to you and the Medical Protection Society.'

We walked to the car and I was about to get in the driver's seat when Daniel asked me to go round to the other side and get in the front passenger's seat.

'When the coroner asked me to leave the courtroom, did he discuss any matters in private with the lawyers?' I said, in the car, wanting to find out more.

'No,' said Catherine. 'Everything that was said was in the full hearing of the whole court. Admittedly it was all in legalese. References were made to Article this, Clause that, and so on, but everyone heard. He also mentioned manslaughter and protecting the witness, but I do not understand why you were not there to hear it. Your lawyer did not raise any objections.'

We drove home in silence.

Chapter Five

30 November 2010

A month after the inquest, in light of the decision of the coroner to refer my case to the CPS, I was summoned to appear again in front of the GMC. This time the meeting was in Manchester, where the GMC was now housed, a few doors down from a row of coffee shops, a supermarket and a sandwich bar. Catherine and I arrived and took the lift to the seventh floor. While we waited, I googled to see who was appearing in front of the regulator that day: all were doctors like myself, with foreign names.

The accusation that a larger proportion of ethnic doctors was being investigated by the GMC was one I had heard levelled for years; nothing seemed to have changed. At least an acknowledgment by the GMC that this disparity existed and was causing disquiet among foreign doctors would have gone some way to address the concerns, but none had been made. As before, the GMC was still acting as accuser and judge, something that was set to change in the course of time.

We were now forced to wait two and a half hours until my case was called. The council had asked for a report from a general surgeon, Mr John Drury, who again made no reference to the patient's original case notes, but only to the Empey report in regurgitated form, in contravention of the GMC's own rules. GMC rules clearly state that no expert should make a judgment on a case based on the conclusions by others and he must refer to original notes on which to base his conclusions. In spite of this the GMC now accepted Mr Drury's opinion on this case and proceeded to put conditions on my licence preventing me from doing any private work.

I could do NHS work only at Ealing Hospital under supervision by my medical director.

This decision would be reviewed every three months and further determinations considered as the case unfolded.

They would notify me of future hearings.

The hospital was happy for me to continue to perform all my NHS work, including taking part in on-call duties and managing emergency admissions.

+ + +

The police now decided to interview me, not as a witness, but as a potential defendant.

Of all the professional bodies to which I belonged, the indemnity body, the MPS, would provide me with the most support; I would now make several visits to the MPS for advice. I was naive enough to believe that the other organisations to which I was a fully paid-up member, including the Royal Colleges of Surgeons and the BMA, would offer assistance at this time of need. I did not expect them to get involved in the legal process, nor did I think it was their place to do so, but I was hoping for psychological support. I knew of reports of other surgeons who had been investigated for manslaughter, some of whom were charged, tried and either acquitted or convicted. Nearly all surgeons were members of one of the Colleges of Surgeons and of the BMA and it was likely that they too would have sought the sort of assistance I was looking for. These were the obvious places to look, away from the workplace, where confidentiality could not be guaranteed.

One morning I rang the switchboard of the Royal College of Surgeons of England. When the woman at the switchboard answered the phone, I explained briefly that a patient had died under my care and I was undergoing difficult investigations that were completely new to me. I had surmised that someone in the college or known to the college would help.

'As far as I'm aware there's no dedicated department or individual for handling such issues, but I'll put you through to someone who can get more details and perhaps find a fellow who could advise you,' she said.

I waited about five minutes and when I did speak to someone, it was a man who asked me detailed questions about my patient and the events leading to his death. Then he started asking a series of questions. As the questions continued, I told him this was *not* what I was looking for and I would appreciate it if I could talk to a surgeon who had knowledge of legal issues to help with writing medical reports and advise on how to participate in police interviews. I also informed him that I needed pastoral and psychological help.

He sighed and asked me to hang on and he would talk to another person who could offer assistance. Another five minutes passed while I listened to a piece of classical music. The next man proceeded to initiate a similar conversation with me. By the time I got through to the third person, it was clear I was not going to get the help I was looking for.

I was in a mess, it was serious and had nothing to do with the college, was the attitude.

I tried the Royal College of Surgeons of Edinburgh, of which I was a fellow, and the BMA, of which I was a member, and they did no better.

The MPS, however, appointed a firm of solicitors to handle my case and the solicitor assigned to help me accompanied me to Harrow Police Station. It was now nearly eleven months since the inquest and almost ten months from my appearance before GMC, but even in this time I was constantly reminded about this case. Nonetheless, the details of the events over the time I cared for Mr Hughes had begun to fade. My family came with me but were not allowed inside the police station. Instead, they were forced to wait in coffee bars in the adjacent shopping complexes while I was interviewed.

Harrow Police Station, 20 and 26 September 2011

We were shown into an interview room where a tape recorder had been set up. I was cautioned that I did not have to say anything but anything I did say would be taken down and used in evidence in the event of a trial; if there was anything that I would later depend on in my defence, which I did not mention in this interview, it would be discounted. One of the detectives interviewing me made me repeat this caution to ensure that I understood it. This was not an invitation to take tea with the police officers but involved questioning me to the point of near breakdown. It was also an opportunity for the interrogators to enhance their careers: a successful prosecution could see a detective constable conducting an interview like this promoted to a higher rank. The officers were more than aggressive, they were downright hostile. The tone of their voices and their body language made it clear to me this was not going to be an easy environment in which to present my case.

I have since discovered that it is best not to commit to an oral interview. Under the stress of the occasion, and unable to consult notes and previous records, a person is liable to make statements that could prove inaccurate. Instead it's best to get the police to provide written questions to which a person can provide written answers, enabling them to check every word for accuracy and seek legal advice before finally submitting a report.

It transpired that I did make mistakes in some of the answers I gave during nearly nine hours of interrogation; the entire transcript would be read in court and analysed forensically to make a case that I was a liar.

+ + +

Over the course of the next two days, over which the interview was conducted, I would discover that I was being investigated for perjury as well as manslaughter. The alleged perjury related to a statement I had made during the coroner's inquest regarding the timing of my viewing of the CT scan result.

The interview went on well into the night on the first day. It was only when the solicitor accompanying me raised objections by pointing out that evidence obtained after such prolonged questioning might not be admissible that the officers saw fit to terminate proceedings and to arrange for me to come back six days later.

'They should prosecute, if that is their intention, not persecute,' said a senior lawyer friend of mine, an eminent barrister from Nigeria whom I would call up later for advice.

By now it was clear to me that the prospects of my case proceeding to prosecution were far greater than at the start.

A defendant facing a manslaughter charge as well as perjury will be charged as a liar; every word they utter will be scrutinised for accuracy. Moreover, perjury can carry more severe punishment than involuntary manslaughter.

Saturday 22 October 2011, 9 a.m.

It was four weeks now since my interview by the police. I was getting ready to go and do my ward round at Ealing Hospital when the doorbell rang. Catherine was out shopping. I was alone in the house and still in my dressing gown. I opened the door expecting the postman, who sometimes delivered mail at this time on a Saturday.

'Are you David Sellu?'

A smartly dressed woman in her forties, looking slightly the worse for wear, shoved a recording device at me.

'Er. Yes,' I said.

'*Sunday Mirror.* I've been informed that you have been interviewed by the police on a possible charge of manslaughter. I would like to invite your comments on this.'

I stared at her in horror.

What now hit me was a combination of intense rage and bewilderment. How did she know about my case, and who had given her my address? What right did she have to confront me in my own house at a time like this?

'I do not wish to talk to you about this case or anything else,' I managed before slamming the door and locking it.

'I take it you do not wish to comment on this matter?' was her parting shot.

In the sitting room I collapsed onto the settee, and found myself next looking at my watch an hour later, feeling numb, as I tried to take in the significance of the encounter. Unable to go to the hospital that morning, I postponed my ward round until the afternoon.

That Sunday a story appeared in the *Sunday Mirror* in which it was reported that I had been interviewed by the police on suspicion of manslaughter.

Was it coincidental that my interview papers and all the results of the witness interviews relating to this case were submitted to the CPS just two days later?

Someone, somewhere, was passing confidential information to the press.

Nobody seemed to have any information, words of advice or reassurance. Even the lawyers were not forthcoming on what to expect. My family were very supportive but these were anxious times. My children visited us more frequently and encouraged me to stay strong. Catherine took me for long walks and made sure I was eating well and getting adequate sleep. None of my colleagues at work really understood the trauma. Perhaps I should have taken some time off work but I knew I would spend it worrying about the outcome of the case and so I decided to continue to work. I would start a major operation wondering what would happen if something went wrong, even the things that go wrong in the hands of all surgeons at the best of times. This was not a good time for me.

If a patient of mine suffered a complication, would this too be held against me and used in a trial, if there was one?

I had read that doctors facing investigation by the GMC were at high risk of taking their own lives. I imagine that those who, in addition, were under police scrutiny are even more vulnerable. I have never considered taking my own life, for I feel this would break my family, but I can understand easily the pressures that drive those who did die by their own hands over the edge.

I consulted a colleague, a consultant clinical psychologist, who was enormously kind and helpful. He taught me relaxation exercises and how to access the right frame of mind to confront the anxious months ahead. Rather than try and forget these problems, it was better to face them in small doses in order to reduce the traumatic stress. Easier said than done. Playing in the back of my mind were the events following the patient's death, the police interviews, and my suspension from the Clementine Churchill Hospital (after several years' unblemished service).

July 2012

I received a call from my solicitor to inform me that the CPS had now considered all the evidence gained from the extensive investigations they had carried out and were asking the police to give me a verdict. Unsettled by the uncertainties that lay ahead, I had been warned by my solicitor that at this juncture, if I was charged, I could be arrested. She was unsure what that would entail and whether I would be placed in a police cell until bailed or possibly remanded in custody. The medical director at Ealing Hospital had previously let it be known that in the event of a charge, the Trust Board had no option but to apply the customary sanction, which was to suspend me from work until the outcome of the trial.

On the appointed day I arrived back at Harrow Police Station accompanied by my solicitor, my wife and two of our children. The solicitor was a white woman in her late fifties and she had short, blond curly hair. Escorted along a dimly lit corridor past dingy police cells, I glanced at the solicitor, whose expression told me to expect the worst. A male junior detective and his more senior colleague, a woman, met us. The atmosphere and their approach was everything I had been trained *not* to bring to bear when giving bad news to my patients. Their body language and the silence made me feel they had no concern for my feelings or psychological well-being. When they gave me the news, there was no preamble

'The CPS have asked me to charge you on two counts: the manslaughter of Mr Hughes on 14 February 2010 and perjury in a coroner's court on 18 October 2010. You don't have to say anything...' the male detective said without emotion.

I looked at my solicitor for what to do and she signalled to me to say nothing.

'Is Mr Sellu going to be arrested?' she asked.

'No, he is not, but he will be required to attend Hendon Magistrates' Court for a formal charge. We will not place any conditions on him at the moment but if he does not show up or if he fails to comply with any of our requests, we know where he will be and we will go and get him,' said the senior detective.

+ + +

Nothing in my life could have prepared me for this moment. In 1991, brutal civil war broke out in Sierra Leone, lasting eleven years. My father died, mercifully, before it started, but my mother and the rest of my family were caught up in it. Some of them were killed and some severely injured, with no functioning medical service. They were forced to live in the bush to escape marauding rebels bent on killing, maiming, raping and destroying property.

I had done the best I could to send them money to ease some of their physical suffering, but I could do nothing about the psychological scars they had endured. For many years, I, too, suffered post-traumatic stress on account of my powerlessness and guilt. My mother died of a stroke shortly after the war was over and my family believed it was probably a result of the trauma inflicted on her during the strife.

I had surmounted these and other difficulties in life but there was nothing I could remember that matched this. Manslaughter, I was informed, carried a maximum sentence of life in prison and if it was compounded with a conviction of perjury, I could remain in prison for the rest of my days.

I had trained to be a doctor, devoted myself to studying and working hard to specialise as a surgeon. I had made it against all the odds. My motivation was to help people. Some of my patients would come back to tell me how they owed their lives to my skills and these expressions of gratitude had meant a great deal to me. However, none of these could compensate for the hurt I was now going through.

+ + +

The medical director at my NHS hospital had warned me that if I were to be charged, I would certainly be suspended from work, but would that mean I would lose my job? I didn't think so. After all, I had not been found guilty of any crime. What would happen to my wife and children in such an eventuality? We had a mortgage on our house and there were other bills to pay. There was so much we took for granted in life. Our children were still struggling to find their feet in the prevailing job market and we had been doing our best to support them, not just financially but psychologically, as they went through the difficult times. Who was going to look after them? Who would care for my patients in Ealing Hospital? I had long given up work at the private hospital and written to all the patients undergoing treatment under me to tell them I was transferring their care to other colleagues if they wanted. They were free to seek help from other surgeons of their choice, of course. I had promised them I would be back, but I knew deep down that even if I was cleared of this charge it was going to be difficult for me to get back into private medicine. I had built up a big practice over the years. Now it was crumbling.

Chapter Six

19 July 2012

Events in the office of the chief executive (CEO) at Ealing, my NHS hospital, and at the next GMC hearing in Manchester were, it turned out, unexpectedly connected. Two days after I was charged, I went to see the CEO to explain to her the events in the police station. The deputy to the medical director was brought in to assist her. The CEO and the medical director perform different functions: the former largely controls the administration of the hospital, while the latter supervises medical matters. Catherine who, in the words of the CEO, 'attended in the capacity of a work colleague', accompanied me.

I presumed work colleagues were allowed at such meetings, whereas wives were not.

Owing to the serious nature of the charges, the CEO decided to exclude me from duty 'on an immediate basis'. This was initially for a period of four weeks to be followed by a review. She went on: 'Exclusion does not constitute disciplinary action, is a neutral act and is without prejudice to any further decisions which the Trust may take, and is on full pay. I advise that whilst excluded from work, you are not permitted to enter the Trust's premises without permission from me or the medical director...'

This last point was particularly hurtful. Of all the hospitals in which I had worked throughout my medical career, Ealing Hospital was where I had spent the most time. I trained

here as a registrar and I was appointed in 1993, some nineteen years earlier. I recalled the hundreds of times I had come
into the premises at all hours of day and night and even spent
whole nights there when I was looking after sick or seriously
wounded patients. And now, I was not allowed in without
permission. I felt hurt and humiliated as we left to go home.

+ + +

The first order restricting my practice was at my second
GMC hearing on 30 November 2010, following the coroner's inquest. This order was reviewed in May 2011, October
2011, February 2012 and May 2012. I had been summoned
to these review meetings but elected, following advice from
my solicitor, not to attend but instead accede to the conditions being maintained. In any case it was unlikely that the
conditions would be changed in the absence of further devel-
opments in the case.

There was now a development, namely, that the police
had charged me with gross negligence manslaughter and
perjury just nine days earlier, and the GMC wasted no time
calling me to Manchester for a further review. From my
experience in the course of this case I had come to realise
that GMC hearings were dehumanising and traumatic.

The way cases were handled by the GMC changed in
June 2012 when a new body, the Medical Practitioners
Tribunal Service, was established in an attempt to answer
the long-levied criticism that the GMC was prosecuting,
judging and sentencing doctors reported to it for misconduct. Under the new arrangement, the GMC would continue
to set the standards that the profession was held to, and
prosecute those who transgressed. The MPTS would take

over the function of judging and deciding on and policing the sanctions imposed. In order to establish a clear line of separation from the GMC, the MPTS established its own offices separate from the regulator. It was to be noted that while the MPTS reported to Parliament, it was funded by the GMC and reported also to the GMC. Many doctors saw this as merely a cosmetic exercise and that the MPTS was an arm of the GMC in all but name.

+ + +

Catherine and I went to Manchester late the night before and had a Chinese takeaway with James, my son, who was in his final year of medical school. We had an early night and got to the venue at about 8.30 a.m. as instructed. We had no information about when my case would be heard and it was not until the afternoon that someone came and ushered us into the large hall where the committee had convened. Nothing seemed to have changed as far as delays were concerned. Once again, I spoke only to say my name and to recite my GMC number, rather like prison where, as I was to discover later, you are known only by your surname and number.

I expected the verdict and I believed that the hearing was merely a formality.

'If the CPS has decided to prosecute,' the legal assessor explained, 'they will have done so in the interest of the public and because there is a realistic chance of conviction.'

The panel went on to hear cases argued by the GMC, on the one hand, for suspension of my registration and by my barrister, on the other, for me to remain on the register with the current conditions, pending the outcome of the case in the courts. In the circumstances, the panel decided to suspend my name from the register, thus barring me from any form of medical practice. In their written statement the MPTS said:

> 'The panel has taken account of the principle of proportionality and has balanced the need to protect members of the public, the public interest and your own interest against the consequences for you of the suspension of your registration. The Panel noted in particular Mr Jenkins's [my barrister's] submission that, if the Interim Order Panel (IOP) were to suspend your registration today the Trust may dispense with your services entirely. Whilst the Panel notes that its order has removed your ability to practise medicine it considers that, in view of the seriousness of the allegations against you, in this case, the interests of patients weigh more heavily than your own interests. In all circumstances it considers that the suspension of your registration is an appropriate response.'

Not surprisingly, I received a letter from the CEO at Ealing Hospital just a few days later to say that my contract at Ealing Hospital had been terminated. The reason given was that I was no longer on the medical register and so, technically, I was not a registered doctor.

I have reproduced this part of the MPTS report into my case for two reasons: first, while I had been charged with criminal offences, I had not been found guilty of any of them. The principle in English law, surely, was innocent until proved guilty in a court of law. Second, as circumstances were to turn out later, this suspension spelled the beginning of a process that would prove irreversible, even if the case against me were to fail in the courts.

13 August 2012

In English law, nearly all criminal court cases start in a magistrates' court. The more serious alleged offences will then be passed to the crown court either for sentencing after the defendant has been found guilty or for full trial with a judge and jury. The magistrate's court can decide on bail issues as it sees fit, prior to transferring a case on to the crown court.

Hendon Magistrates' Court was located on the high street in a busy northwest London suburb and Catherine and I visited the day before the hearing. It was a difficult place to drive to and we wanted to see if there was convenient parking in the vicinity. We found a large supermarket car park just across the road from the court. News of my impending charge had reached many of my colleagues and I received several phone calls on the day of the hearing from colleagues expressing good wishes.

We arrived early on the Monday morning and were surprised to see many of the detectives who had been involved in my case doing their grocery shopping before they walked to court. I did not know them but my solicitor who was with me, Catherine and James, pointed them out by name.

About forty-five minutes or so before my case was due to be heard we decided to walk to the court building. As we crossed the road and stepped on the pavement on the court side of the road the solicitor, who was walking next to me with Catherine and James, gave me a nudge and said: 'Photographers – just continue to walk and pretend not to notice them.'

The woman standing by a camera on a tripod, some thirty yards from us, put her mobile phone away and I guessed someone who recognised me had told her who I was. She swung into action behind a huge telephoto lens and pointed the camera straight at us, and as she was standing close to the only entrance into the building we had no choice but to come within feet of where she was. I could hear the camera whirring away and she must have taken scores of shots of us.

My wife and son were clearly distressed by this intrusion and they walked closer to me. I did not notice James place his hand on my shoulder – I noticed this only after I saw the picture on the internet some time later. My picture had never appeared in the newspapers or online and I was worried about how much more the press would intrude in our lives. I was concerned too about the negative publicity my family would be subjected to for events in which they had taken no part and the prospect of this denying me a fair trial.

I recognised the police officers who had interviewed me, and there were several other people there with notepads and laptops, no doubt journalists, reporting on the cases that day. It did not take long to confirm my suspicion about who was passing information about my identity to the photographer stationed outside. When I looked back the way we came in, I could see the photographer with her equipment and the location we were at when she turned her attention to us was clearly visible.

I was summoned into the dock, or more precisely a cage into which I was locked. My name and date of birth were read out and I was asked to state my address before the two charges were read out. I pleaded not guilty. I was given unconditional bail and the trial was listed to take place at the Old Bailey in October 2013.

The photographer was there again as we walked out of court and this time she did not need anyone to instruct her who to look out for. Our solicitor walked a discreet distance behind my family and me thereby absenting herself from the not very flattering pictures that would appear in the press. This was a foretaste of what was to come.

2 October 2013

One of the most disturbing aspects of my trial was the role of the expert witnesses for the prosecution. Firstly, it was not for them to say what they would do or what was ideal in a given clinical situation; what would a responsible body of surgeons in my position do, or not do, was what they should have been asked. Secondly, the standards against which to judge a practitioner are the standards that prevail at the time of the incident (a survey conducted just a year after Mr Hughes died showed that what I did was standard practice in the majority of hospitals in the UK).

It was also evident that some issues were too complex for a lay jury; some of the issues fell outside the experts' field of expertise and they (the experts) explained them badly.

The exchange below, between the prosecuting barrister and one of the experts for the prosecution, Mr Michael Kelly, is taken from the notes of a junior solicitor in the legal firm instructing my barrister; I, too, took notes:

Prosecuting barrister: 'What is the effect of CT scan on someone with this condition? What will it show you?'

Expert: 'Page three of the glossary gives you the definition of CT scan. It works by taking a whole series of focussed cuts of the abdomen. When you look at it on a screen, you can go up and down looking at it – all the way from the diaphragm to the pelvis. The radiologist can do it in two planes, horizontal and vertical. It's tricky, I really need a bit of guidance from a radiologist. In this context, it will show you abnormalities in the sigmoid colon, fluid that has come out, known as a collection. The free gas which is now obvious, and certain additional spin-offs, in that you can see the other organs and see if they look normal, for example the liver. The radiologist will tell you other bits are normal, so when you get to operation, that is your background.'

He paused for a while and then continued:

'With regard to diverticulitis, it will show you whether the gas and bacteria are going into the root of the sigmoid. It will also show if it has gone behind the peritoneal cavity – called retroperitoneal gas. The definition is in the glossary on page nine. Getting into that is bad. CT scan also tells you if there are any other collections of pus. In a case of short duration such as this patient, it is not very likely but it reassures you when you operate that you don't have to make extensive searches for other collections. It will also show you alternative diagnoses if you get the plain X-ray wrong, for example in this type of case, blockage to the main arteries of the intestine, a condition known as mesenteric infarction. Infarction is defined on page six of the glossary. This is important, as this requires a different kind of operation. But if there is free gas, this is not on the radar.'

Prosecuting barrister: 'What is the treatment of a perforation?'

Expert: 'If there is free perforation, the patient will need an operation. The purpose of the operation is to do something about the hole and to clean out the peritoneal cavity.'

Prosecuting barrister: 'What can be done about the hole?'

Expert: 'Remove part of the sigmoid colon which has the hole. You can either join the bowel together or you can stitch up the far end going up to the rectum and bring the other end out to the abdominal wall as a colostomy or a bag. Then there is the potential of re-operating to put things back together again.

'Of these two, the disconnection is called Hartmann's operation (explained on page five of the glossary), while the joining up together is a primary anastomosis (page one of glossary). Hartmann's is the safer of the two because it is less likely to leak. A number of primary anastomoses will leak. The leakage rate is 5 per cent.

'An initial consideration in the case of Mr Hughes is the knee. The knee had a significant bruise and you can easily lose half a litre to one litre of blood into the bruise. Bruises are susceptible to being colonised by bacteria in the blood. This causes an infection in the bruise. Orthopaedic surgeons are fearful of this, as the bruise is in direct contact with the metal of the knee. The end result is that you have to take out the metal. In this particular case the last thing you want is for the anastomosis to leak.'

This expert witness was even prepared to make wild speculation with no evidence to back it.

Prosecuting barrister: 'Had scan been carried out on the evening of 11, what would it have shown?' (11 refers to Thursday 11 February, the date on which I first saw Mr Hughes.)

Expert: 'It would not have been as bad. Free air, a bit of a collection of fluid but none of the retroperitoneal air or artery tracking.'

When asked to comment on the liver tests the patient had undergone, the following misleading statements were made by this expert, even though he was no liver specialist.

'Bilirubin: this is an indication of liver failure; gamma GT: this protein is secreted by the liver and is an indication of liver being in trouble; albumin is low – it is a good general marker of physiological well-being and as you get sicker, it goes down.

'This CT report does not mention any liver issues, therefore he cannot have seen cirrhosis of the liver.'

There was even a suggestion that liver damage had occurred because of the delay in the operation and in response, Mr Kelly said:

'The reason for the liver damage is clotting derangement.'

When asked to summarise my role in the management of Mr Hughes, this was what Mr Kelly said, in language that was wholly inappropriate for an expert in a criminal court:

'Mr Sellu owed Mr James Hughes a duty of care from when he took over his care and he breached this duty of care.

'During the whole of that night and the next day he embarked on a slow, laid-back and inadequate treatment regimen which would not pass a students' final examination.

'In my opinion this was an almost completely avoidable death, the predicted POSSUM mortality on the first night being two to three per cent. Sellu's performance amounted to reckless gross negligence and this had a major decisive influence on Mr Hughes's death.'

Alarmed by these outrageous statements, my barrister questioned this expert witness about his partiality. The following were the exchanges:

Defence barrister: 'Do you accept that the test for a proper and fair criticism of Mr Sellu's clinical management is to determine if his actions were reasonable, as opposed to ideal?'

Expert: 'Yes.'

Defence barrister: 'And you as an expert must judge his actions on a prospective basis?'

Expert: 'Yes.'

Defence barrister: 'Will you refrain from judging his actions with regard to what we now know?'

Expert: 'Yes.'

Defence barrister: 'Will you judge him on the basis of what was then available to him?'

Expert: 'Yes.'

Defence barrister: 'After the event, do you accept that reconstruction is a very dangerous route indeed?'

Expert: 'Yes.'

Defence barrister: 'And in determining whether this doctor acted reasonably, will you agree to consider that some doctors might take a different view or route?'

Expert: 'Yes.'

Defence barrister: 'And the fact that some doctors might take a different view or different route does not make him guilty of negligence?'

Expert: 'That's correct.'

Despite these assurances, however, this expert was not prepared to change his stance.

It was also wrong for experts to judge my alleged actions or inactions to be 'grossly negligent'. On a number of occasions they were spurred on by the prosecuting barrister. It was the job of the jury, not the experts, to determine whether I was grossly negligent, this being the ultimate question they had to deliberate on.

The judge failed to make that clear.

In my view the judge should have disallowed the experts straying into fields that were outside their areas of practice.

The chances of Mr Hughes dying after a major operation, for example, were put by the prosecution medical experts at 2.6 per cent and took no account of all his background medical conditions and his recent major operation. Yet the testimonies of the two prosecution experts, who were not specialist statisticians, were accepted without challenge. It was obvious to me that his mortality risk was at least 30 per cent and this is based on the fact that once a patient perforates their bowel, they have a one-in-three chance of dying, however well they are treated. I had mentioned this several times to my legal team, but it was ignored. What raised this risk even further were the major operation he had only five days earlier and his liver cirrhosis.

During my trial Mr Michael Kelly, one of the prosecution experts, also gave opinions about Mr Hughes's liver cirrhosis, a subject that was again clearly outside his field of expertise. The judge took everything Mr Kelly said as fact and without question. At one point in my testimony I disagreed with a point Mr Kelly had made and the judge, surprised, interrupted to ask if I was contradicting what Mr Kelly had said. I said, respectfully, yes, I was. Experts, we all recognised, were merely expressing opinions and could be wrong. Mr Kelly said that I had exhibited a 'laid-back attitude' in the management of the patient under my care. This was never defined and was even used by the judge to describe my actions in his sentencing remarks.

Chapter Seven

5 *November 2013*

The jury were out.

Every day Catherine and I would say goodbye to each other before we reached the entrance. We were aware that if I was found guilty there was every probability that I'd be led away to prison immediately. We discussed practical matters, almost Dickensian in their matter-of-factness, such as what I should wear, how much money to carry in my pocket and whether to bring a bag of personal effects in the event that I was incarcerated. What would I put in it? What about debit and credit cards?

Looking back, it was astonishing that I was given no advice or guidance on this.

In the event, I wore a suit, as I had each day throughout the trial, a tie and prescription glasses. I had a small amount of money and my usual shopping cards. I did not carry a bag but I had my notebook and pen used to make notes throughout the trial.

In medicine we are required to explain and justify the paths to diagnoses and decisions, as these may be life changing. If a surgeon makes a diagnosis of say, colon cancer, it is because they have found a lump on the bowel, taken a sample from it and had it examined by a pathologist; the pathologist in turn would describe the features of the cells and their constituents and the ways in which they differ from normal. If the pathologist makes a cancer diagnosis, they have to determine how serious that cancer is based on the degree to which the cancerous cells differ from normal; this is known as grading. They also determine whether the cancer is still localised to the part of the bowel from which it arose or has spread to the lymph nodes that drain that part of the bowel. The surgeon will do other tests such as CT scans to see whether or not the cancer has spread to other parts of the body such as the liver and lungs. Whether the cancer has spread to lymph nodes or distant organs is referred to as staging.

The ways in which a patient with a given cancer is treated depend, among other factors, on the grade and stage of the cancer. The prognosis, or the outlook for the patient, will be inferred from this information. For instance, a tumour with a poor grade that has spread to distant organs has a worse prognosis than one with a good grade that has not spread. Everyone in this process will be highly trained, certified to be skilled and will have had experience making these decisions. They will be held responsible if the diagnosis proves to be wrong or if the patient dies.

By contrast, the jury in a criminal trial are chosen because they are ordinary people; it would be undesirable, it is argued, for expert knowledge to interfere with the way in which they make their judgment. All they have to deliver is a 'guilty' or 'not guilty' verdict to a charge but are protected by law from divulging how they reached the verdict. They have no responsibility if they get the verdict wrong.

+ + +

Waiting for the verdict was a nail-biting experience. I sat with my lawyers in an office outside the courtroom and they engaged in small talk to try to pass the time. The verdict could take an hour or two or several days and the jury had been told they had as much time as they wished to come to a decision. Every time the tannoy crackled into life, my heart would race (despite my beta-blocking drugs) and I would listen intently to what was being said, in case it was a call for us to return to my courtroom.

Then came the call for us to return to Court 1.

We would all take our usual places.

The jury, it was evident, were struggling trying to understand my case. On the first day of their deliberation the jury came to court to announce that one of their members was suffering unbearable stress and they all wanted to be dismissed for the day, which they were. On the second day, they sent a note to the judge saying: *Two questions: one could we please be reminded of what we must or are deliberating on (evidence)? Two, are we to be deliberating legalities or are to be judging as human beings, lay people?* (Sic)

Rather than give clear precise answers to these questions, the judge merely repeated the directions he had previously given. On the third day the jury came back informing the judge that they had reached a verdict on one of the charges but could not reach a unanimous verdict on the second. The judge informed them he would accept a majority verdict. We went back out again as I waited anxiously, not knowing whether to sit still or pace up and down. I looked at my lawyers for guidance but was too afraid to ask their opinion on what the final verdicts might be. They did not offer any advice but I noted that the junior barrister had brought in a large tome, *Banks on*

Sentence, and left it on the table. Were they trying to tell me something?

I was terrified.

+ + +

'Would everyone involved in proceedings in Court 1 please make their way to the courtroom,' came the announcement.

The number of people who streamed into the courtroom seemed to have quadrupled over the course of the trial. Many people were now forced to stand.

I found myself standing between two prison warders standing guard; the second one had a pair of handcuffs.

Those of us with seats were alerted to get to our feet with two taps heralding the words, 'Court rise.'

Judge Nicol took his seat.

The head juror was asked to stand and an official on the judge's podium reminded him that there were two charges, perjury and gross negligence manslaughter.

'Would the defendant stand up,' I was commanded.

'Do you find the accused guilty or not guilty of the first charge, perjury?' he addressed the head juror.

'Not guilty.'

Relief.

'Do you find the accused guilty or not guilty of gross negligence manslaughter?'

'Guilty.'

'Did you say, guilty of manslaughter?' the official enquired.

'Yes.'

I was cleared of perjury but found guilty of manslaughter by a majority of ten to two – the minimum required to convict.

I felt nothing. The adrenaline that had sustained me for nearly four years now vanished, leaving me in a state that I can only describe as emotional paralysis.

The court adjourned; the judge retired to consider the sentence.

I had little doubt that a change in the law just a few years earlier almost certainly mandated a prison sentence. Prior to 2012 most of the doctors convicted of gross negligence received suspended sentences, but a change in sentencing guidelines had resulted in all three doctors convicted between 2012 and 2013 being sent to prison (all of an ethnic minority background despite constituting only 20 per cent of the workforce).

+ + +

'You may remain seated for the time being,' he started.

After Judge Justice Andrew Nicol delivered his sentencing remarks, which were broadcast around the word, I thought the extreme humiliation could not get worse.

'David Sellu, the jury have found you guilty of the manslaughter of Jim Hughes because of gross negligence while he was under your care and you were his consultant surgeon.'

He went on to outline the case the prosecution had put before the jury, which they said they did not understand and on which they had found me guilty. He continued:

'In summary, I am satisfied that the Crown has proved to the necessary standard, each of the aspects of gross negligence which they alleged.'

Had they?

'Even if you had acted more speedily, there was a chance Mr Hughes would have died anyway. There is always such a risk with major abdominal surgery of the kind which he needed...'

Well, well, I thought to myself, *and you still say I was responsible for his death?*

Then, referring to the Empey report, this was what he said:

'I have considered the cases and statutory provisions which the prosecution have drawn to my attention. I accept that in your case there was no alteration of medical records which would have been a significantly aggravating factor. However, in your witness statements for the coroner and your answers to Professor Empey's investigation you made numerous errors. All of them put you in a better light. It is true, as your counsel has said, that you were charged with no offence in relation to these matters and the jury has acquitted you of count two on the indictment. However, at the very least they show a lack of candour with those responsible for investigating Mr Hughes' death.'

I wonder what this judge would now say if he knew that the Empey report was embellished and hid all the faults uncovered in the RCA? Moreover, for a matter of this complexity, dragging on as it had for nearly four years, it was inevitable that inconsistencies in witness statements had crept in. Some witnesses had exonerated themselves by simply responding that they did not remember.

'You are sixty-six years old and a man without previous convictions or cautions and, of course, I take that into account.

'I have heard the evidence of Dr Whitehead, who praised your ability and dedications as a surgeon. I have read the references from your many colleagues in the NHS and private practice who speak equally highly of your skill and care for patients. This case is completely at odds with that picture. There is no explanation as to why it should have been so...'

He told me this was the end of my career and spoke of the impact this case would have on me and my family.

'Stand up.

'David Sellu, for the offence of unlawfully killing James Hughes you are sentenced to two and a half years' imprisonment.'

+ + +

'How long did he give you?' the guard asked as we walked down the cold staircase to the basement.

'Two and a half years,' I said, trying hard to suppress my tears.

'That's not so bad. Look on the bright side,' he replied cheerily, 'the last chap I took down got twenty-two years. You'll be out in just fifteen months.'

Bright side? Just fifteen months?

Later, when I came to read Jeffrey Archer's account of his journey from the dock to the cells of the Old Bailey in *A Prison Diary Volume 1 Hell*, I realised that prison guards said this to all convicted defendants as a matter of course. The guard makes the sentence sound like a short break, a holiday, away from work. Locked in a cell, I was pleased to see my barrister and solicitor who arrived shortly afterwards. They promised they would see my family the next day and give them some assurance.

'You won't be in for long,' the barrister explained. 'The prison system does not like professional people like you on their hands. You should be moved to an open prison within two or three weeks and released on an electronic tag in about six months.'

This was the good news. The bad news was that he saw no grounds for appealing my conviction or sentence and gave no reason for why he had reached this conclusion.

Too traumatised to say anything, I nodded.

This barrister had described me during our meetings as *diffident* and I was not sure how to take this. Many of my patients had commented that they found my non-aggressive demeanour a welcome change from that of other gung-ho surgeons they encountered. But a lawyer colleague had warned me that if I lost my case, I must refrain from arguing with my defence barrister about an appeal. The barrister would see an appeal as a failure on their part to defend my case adequately.

But I couldn't help thinking,

What about the way the case was conducted? And how medical issues had been oversimplified to a lay jury? Did he really consider Mr Kelly a credible expert witness? The jury said they did not understand the charge, and yet they received no adequate direction. The judge had used parts of the Empey report to prove my culpability but he did not question the credentials and impartiality of those who conducted the investigation and ruled on its findings. Was I being fairly judged against the prevailing standards of prac-tice at the time?

My answer would be no.

Chapter Eight

I was transported from the Old Bailey to prison in what is referred to as a *prisoner transport vehicle*, or a prison on wheels. You have probably seen photographers running after prison vans, pointing their cameras at the windows in an attempt to get pictures of high-profile detainees. I'd been led to the prison van waiting in the courtyard, handcuffed to a lady prison officer, cigarette in one hand, dragging me along with her other hand to make sure I kept up. I now found myself locked up in this sweatbox, behind a thick door with a glass panel that allowed staff to view the prisoner without opening the door. The walls were reinforced and there was a tiny window with views to the street outside. Stuffed into the cramped sweatbox on a metal seat, scanning the street through the tinted window, I found myself crying for the first time in years.

What's happened to me?

I was now a common criminal. I'd been found guilty of manslaughter, but this was no ordinary killing.

The dead man was a patient of mine, who along with his family had entrusted his life to me at a time when he was most vulnerable. Not only did I *not* save that life, I took it away. This is the antithesis of medicine, the ultimate violation of the sacred Hippocratic oath. Many doctors, contrary to popular belief, do not swear this oath. Medicine and society have changed enormously since the days of Hippocrates. His oath prohibits practices such as abortion and physician-assisted suicide, which, though controversial, are legal in some countries. At my graduation the dean of my medical school read out to all of us a set of rules, which included doing the best for all of our patients, and emphasised that these were the ideals we were expected to follow when admitted to the medical profession. He shook hands with each graduate and said: 'I admit you.'

I did not swear any oath, but many of the principles of the Hippocratic oath had guided my entire practice since I came into the profession.

I could not get the word *killing* out of my mind. Killing conjured visions of me administering a lethal cocktail of drugs or using a scalpel to decapitate my patient. It filled me with confusion. I had entered the profession to save lives and like every practitioner, I had not always succeeded in doing so. Some deaths cannot be prevented. In this instance, according to the conviction, I had taken the life away. This killing had also violated another maxim, *primum non nocere*, or 'first do no harm'. I had let my patient down on both counts. I felt sorry for him and his family and I knew I would always share their grief.

But was prison the way to punish healthcare workers under whose care patients die, even though these workers had no malice towards those for whom they cared and were not reckless in discharging their duties?

Would medicine ever be able to learn from deaths and non-fatal complications in the same way as the airline industry if such punishments were meted out? In aviation all incidents are thoroughly investigated and where honest mistakes have occurred, lessons are disseminated for all to learn. No one is blamed or threatened and no sanctions are imposed. This does not mean, of course, that criminal action will go unpunished.

Forcing myself not to panic on the long journey to prison, I ran through a list of concerns: My salary had long stopped but I still had bills to pay; I would have no access to my bank account for the next fifteen months and I had to hand over all my bank details to my family to deal with. I was not even sure if the savings I had were going to be enough to sustain my family. Then there was the international humiliation, and I could just imagine the press conference outside the Old Bailey when the members of the CPS would be patting themselves on the back for a successful landmark prosecution and making statements about how dismal my conduct as a surgeon in handling the case of Mr Hughes had been.

No doubt many colleagues I had worked with would be sympathetic, but a handful who saw me as a competitor would not. My family and I were now social outcasts in our community; it would take a long time to repair the damage. We had lived in our house for over twenty years and in that time, we had earned the respect of our neighbours who knew we were healthcare workers. Now what must they think?

+ + +

The prison van stopped. There was a lot of shouting and banging. I heard a key rattle in a few doors and then, *Out*.

I now found myself in front of a large officer I had not met before.

'Belmarsh.'* He greeted us.

Forced to go through a series of metal detectors and X-ray scanners, I was asked to 'open wide' before undergoing a strip search (to my relief, rectal or other internal examinations were not required). This was clearly designed to prevent me and other prisoners bringing contraband items, including drugs, into the prison.

I had come to court that morning dressed in a suit. I had on a watch, and with me my wallet with £120 in £20 notes and the usual bunch of cards, a belt and a pair of spectacles. I also had a notebook and a pen I had brought every day of the trial to record proceedings. In the past I had seen pictures of some savvy defendants coming to court on the day of their sentence with a suitcase, presumably with personal effects in the event of a guilty verdict and an immediate prison sentence. The thought had crossed my mind each time we returned to court while the jury were out considering their verdict. While I was increasingly aware that I would go to prison, I simply could not bring myself to pack a bag to take to court.

I was allowed to keep my watch, underpants, socks, shoes and spectacles but everything else was taken away from me. These items, I was told, would be carefully marked and

---

* Belmarsh is a large prison in Woolwich in the southeast of London, south of the River Thames. It is made up of four three-storey blocks, each further divided into spurs extending from a hub. In prisons a spur is a wing projecting from a central area and ending blindly. All access into or out of a spur is through the central area except in an emergency and there may be two or more spurs to a building. Several layers of brick walls, barbed wire fences and iron gates and a profusion of security cameras surround Belmarsh prison. There are numerous doors with locks: no two doors can be open at the same time. There are numerous criss-crossing corridors. Access to the cells is by steep and narrow staircases.

returned to me when I was finally released from prison. Alternatively, I could apply while in prison to have some or all of them returned to my family. My money was also taken away and the officers told me they would put it into an account for my use in prison. There would be restrictions on how I received and spent the money; this would be explained to me when I got inside. I was given two large transparent carrier bags containing two sets of maroon prison tracksuits, bedding, towels and basic toiletry items such a bar of soap, a toothbrush and toothpaste. I changed into a prison tracksuit and at that point my transformation into a prisoner was complete. I did not need a mirror to know I looked ridiculous; I felt ridiculous. The humiliation from the courtroom was compounded.

I was locked in a room that felt like a refrigerator. The officers were not forthcoming about where I would be going next, so I had to be patient. Over an hour later, a tall officer who would not have looked out of place in the army, opened the door and instructed me to pick up my bags and follow him. We must have gone through a dozen doors before I was told to sit in the corner of the hall and await further instructions.

+ + +

I wondered what was happening to my family. I was still haunted by the sound of Catherine and my children sobbing in the gallery in the Old Bailey. Who did they have to comfort them? How were they going to cope with my incarceration? I recalled the walk that Catherine and I had taken by the canal in Harefield two weekends ago, to discuss the trial and its possible outcome. We had been mildly optimistic that I would be acquitted, that we would be given a chance to pick up where we had left off before this sad affair took place.

What we had not discussed was what life was going to be like for them, my family, if I was sent to prison.

+ + +

An orderly appeared (I later discovered, a prisoner).

'Starter or reception pack? You have a choice between a smoker's pack and a non-smoker's pack,' he said.

I was confused: 'What's this all about?'

'It will take a few days before you get a chance to buy snacks and things for tea and coffee in your cell,' he explained. 'The starter pack has tea, milk, coffee, sugar, toothpaste, toothbrush, biscuits and so on. The smoker's pack also has tobacco and a lighter.' He went on to say: 'I strongly recommend a starter pack. You are going to need it and this is your only opportunity for a good few days to buy anything from the canteen.'

I imagined the canteen as a shop in the prison from which to buy these items.

'Non-smoker's pack, please,' I said without enthusiasm.

'You have to pay for it, but not right away and not in cash. The money will come out of your account. Sign here.'

The pack was handed to me a little while later. I had no desire for food that night but I was grateful to have a drink of tea and I had enough to brush my teeth before I went to bed.

+ + +

The officer who had brought me here now reappeared.

I was startled when he shouted: 'Sellu.'

He gestured for me to follow him to a far corner of the room where there was a phone on the wall.

'You are allowed one phone call and it has to be made to a close family member,' he continued. 'Who do you want to call?'

'My wife, please.'

'OK,' he handed me a piece of paper and a small stubby pen. 'Write the number here.'

I wrote Catherine's mobile phone number.

The officer took the piece of paper from me, dialled the number and handed me the receiver as he stood next to me.

'It's me,' I said.

Catherine told me later that I sounded depressed when I spoke to her on that, my first night in prison, although I'd worked hard not to. I didn't want to drag everybody down by admitting that I was going through the worst day of my life. Despite trying to sound as upbeat as possible, she knew me too well.

'It's really grim and so degrading,' I said, and then, 'How is everybody bearing up?'

'Traumatised, as you can imagine, but we are all together in this and we will see it through.' I was pleased to hear a reassuring voice. 'Tom [her brother] and your brother Denis are coming with me and the children tomorrow to meet the barrister to discuss your case, and I will write about the meeting in detail as soon as it is over.' The digital display on the phone set showed the amount of credit on the officer's account and the numbers were counting down rapidly.

'Have you eaten?'

The officer looked at me and from his wrinkled brow and the gentle shuffle of his feet, I sensed my time was almost up.

'Yes,' I said, without describing the coagulated mess masquerading as vegetable pasta that I had been given.

'Stay strong, we are all in this together and we are behind you. Find out about visiting. We love you very much,' said Catherine, as the officer held out his hand like a parent to a naughty child.

I handed him back the phone and, in exchange, he gave me back the piece of paper with Catherine's phone number.

I went back to my seat.

+ + +

'Follow me.'

I looked at my watch. It was about 9.30 p.m. A younger officer with a beard and glasses who reminded me of Groucho Marx pointed to my bags on the floor. 'Leave those here.'

More doors opened and closed before I was shown into a small dimly lit room.

'Wait here until you are called,' he said.

He locked the door behind him as he walked out.

The opening and locking of doors was a ritual, I was to discover, that staff performed countless times every day. There was no way to escape, I reflected, as I took a seat on a long narrow bench and stared at the pipe running through the walls. This was the heating system.

There was no one else in the room and I closed my eyes, thinking over the events of the day.

About half an hour later, another officer called out 'Sellu,' and escorted me to a room with a sign on the door that read *Doctor*, and for the first time, it began to dawn on me what to expect.

The well-dressed black doctor in a pinstriped suit stood up when I entered, and showed me a seat.

'I am one of the prison medical officers.'

'Hello,' I said, taking the seat.

'What's your name?' he said, from behind the computer screen.

'Sellu,' I replied, 'S-E-L-L-U, David Sellu.'

As he moved the mouse on the table, he asked, 'which court have you come from today?'

'The Old Bailey.'

'OK,' he replied. 'I am going to ask you some questions. Bear with me as I enter the answers into the computer.' He asked me a series of questions, including date of birth, home address, marital status, and then: 'Do you suffer from any illnesses?'

'Yes, I am being treated for blood pressure.'

'What medications are you on?'

'Irbesartan; I can't remember the dose. Bisoprolol 5 mg once daily; I remember the dose because my cardiologist had told me to double the dose from the 2.5 mg I was originally on to try to calm my nerves during the trial. Felodipine 2.5 mg once daily, and Simvastatin 40 mg I think.'

'Smoke?'

'No.'

'Do you drink alcohol?'

'Yes, about fourteen units a week,' wondering what my wife would say if she were here. By the time the trial had started I was drinking in excess of twenty-eight units and Catherine had told me to go easy on alcohol. It was going to be another fifteen months before I was going to be allowed any alcohol and I had prepared myself for this.

'Do you take any drugs? Cocaine, heroin, cannabis?'

'No.'

'Any history of mental illness? Depression, anxiety, schizophrenia?'

'No, but the experience I have been through is enough to make anybody anxious and depressed.'

'I understand. Any history of self-harm?'

'No.'

'What was your occupation?'.

'Doctor.'

'What field?'

'Colorectal surgery,' I said. 'I was a consultant colorectal surgeon.'

He took his hand off the computer mouse and looked at me in interest. I went on to explain briefly the events that led up to my conviction and that I had been given a prison sentence of two and a half years.

'You will be out in fifteen months.'

He then went on to tell me why we should never lose our guard in our profession. He had himself been involved in an incident where he was called to see a disturbed patient and when he got there the patient had already been attended to. Yet when the report was written it stated that he had refused to come out to an urgent call. He was able to defend this accusation successfully, though he could have been in trouble.

'I think you will be all right in a regular cell,' he told me. (A few years earlier, every new prisoner was placed in a 'suicide' cell on their first night.)

Regular cells, I was about to find out, held three inmates: I would have preferred my own cell had I been given a choice.

But in any case I understood it was not up to the doctor to make this decision.

He weighed me, measured by blood pressure and took my pulse and temperature. 'Your blood pressure is raised at 160/108,' he said as he took out a blank pathology request form from a pile on the table.

'Well, I am not surprised. You have had a difficult day. I will arrange for you to have your blood pressure checked twice a day and for blood tests tomorrow.' I felt reassured as he wrote out the requests on the pathology form. 'I will put you on Amlodipine instead of Irbesartan and Felodipine and you can continue on Bisoprolol and Simvastatin.'

Prisoners were not allowed to bring even prescribed medications into prison and any that were brought were confiscated at reception. I had not brought any of my medications and in any case the doctor had decided to change my treatment plan.

'It is going to be difficult for someone of your status but you have to do your best. I am here and if there is any more I can do, feel free to ask the officers to allow you to come and see me,' Dr E said.

Much later, that night, the nurse, accompanied by a prison officer, came to my cell and gave me a week's supply of medicines. 'You must put in an app to get a fresh supply at least two days before you finish this lot,' he informed me.

'Why can't they just supply the medicines in five or six days' time?'

'This is a prison, you know, and we do things our way.'

This was a remark I had not expected to hear from prison staff, who, as I understood it, were charged with providing healthcare to prisoners with the same level of efficiency and compassion as the general population. I was nevertheless encouraged by the encounter with Dr E that night and felt optimistic that at least my medical problems would be one less matter to worry about.

Chapter Nine

I was on Block 3 in a cell at the top of the stairs, on the third landing, at the farthest end. I had a quick glance at the two name cards next to the door. Each showed the name and number of the prisoner, the cell number and the name of the personal officer for that prisoner. It was clear that I was sharing a three-man cell. I waited anxiously for the officer to open the heavy metal door and stand by to let me in before locking the door behind him.

It took me a few minutes for my eyes to adjust.

The cell measured three steps by five steps, obviously designed for two but now accommodating three. There was a single bed on the left-hand wall and a bunk bed on the right. The space between the beds had a small table and chair on the far wall and on that wall were shelves that had clothes, a few books, plastic plates and bowls and plastic cutlery. There was a television and an electric kettle on the table. On the near wall was a washbasin and on the floor beneath it was a large open black bin with leftover food. I discovered later that inmates were locked up in their cells as soon they had collected their food and there was no opportunity for any uneaten food to be discarded outside of the cell till the next day.

Between the single bed and the sink was a tiny cubicle with half a door from ground level and this was the toilet. I could see if there was someone sitting on the toilet. The window behind the television on the far wall had no curtains and had been left partially open in an attempt to clear the air.

The room was cold on that November evening. One of two occupants was lying on the single bed and the other on the lower of the bunk beds. It was obvious that I was to occupy the top bunk.

'Hello,' I said. 'My name's David.'

There was a moment's delay before each said simply said *hello*, adding, I'm John and then Clive.

I was not sure how long they had occupied the cell but I could imagine that having a third person dumped in this tiny space was unwelcome. I pushed one of the two bags I was carrying underneath the bunk bed and left the second in the narrow passage between the beds. There was not a lot of room underneath the beds, with the existing occupants' belongings already deposited there. The second bag had two bed sheets, a blanket and a towel and I proceeded to make the bed I would be sleeping in. The bed sheets were just large enough to tuck under the mattress and it was not hard to figure out that once I got into bed, it would be only a matter of time before the sheets were off the bed. The mattress was a thin piece of hard plastic and the pillow was made of the same material. The head ends of the beds were towards the door: it would be too cold to sleep with your head by the window and moreover, as the TV was on the table, it could only be seen from this position if you were lying in the bed.

Clive, the inmate on the lower bunk bed, got up and cleared one of the shelves on our side of the cell to give me space to place my toiletries and other items. I fished out a toothbrush, toothpaste, bar of soap and a towel. It had been a long day. All I wanted to do was to go to bed, not even knowing or caring whether I would survive until the next day.

Either the shock would kill me or I would die at the hands of another inmate. Deaths in prison were not uncommon.

+ + +

One of the hardest aspects of prison life was being forced to share limited space with people you did not know. I learned much later that in the right environment and with choice and planning, having company could ease the burden of incarceration; it could even provide a solution to being locked up alone for over twenty-two hours a day. But my question was, why was it necessary to share such limited space? Clearly the prison population had outgrown the available space and the only way that prisoners could be accommodated was for them to share cells. In most prisons the majority of cells were designed for single occupancy and a small number to house two inmates. When the prison was overpopulated extra furniture was added to single cells to convert them to double occupancy and cells for two were used to house three prisoners.

Some prisoners believed that forcing them to share cells was a deliberate act of punishment. Arguably, it was a means of optimising the meagre staff numbers given the shortage of officers in almost all prisons; it was easier for them to lock up prisoners in cells if there were fewer cells to manage. Finally, it was desirable for the prison to house some inmates in single cells: prisoners incarcerated for terrorism offences were perceived to have the power to indoctrinate other prisoners and incite unrest. These inmates were kept in single cells to allow prison officers to control their activities. Where there was shortage of accommodation the best way to free up room for these individuals was for other cells to be shared.

Whatever the configuration of cells, it was against the law to compel inmates to eat, sleep and perform toilet functions in the same room, but sadly no one seemed to care.

+ + +

I brushed my teeth, went to the toilet to pass urine and washed my hands. There were going to be several issues to contend with but for now the three most important were how to get into and out of bed, the rules about the single bright fluorescent light on the ceiling just above my bed and the time the TV was to be switched off.

There was a metal stepladder bolted to the foot of the upper bunk with the bottom rung at about chest height. You either had to be an athletic acrobat to get up the ladder, or like me to resort to standing on the one chair available to get a foothold. I got into bed and wanted to go to sleep but the light and the TV were still on. The light switch, I discovered, was just by the door as you came in and whoever switched the light off had to get out of bed to do so.

John was in his mid thirties, a stocky build with a completely shaven head. Clive was perhaps two or three years older than John, of average build and had short cropped blonde hair. They were both lying on their beds and watching a late programme on TV.

'When do we switch the light and the TV off?' I asked wearily as I pulled the bed cover over my head.

'The last person to go to sleep turns the light and the telly off,' said Clive from the bed below. 'Remember you can't get to the light switch or the telly from your bed, so if you are last, you will have to come down and switch it off.'

'Then you have to find your way back in the dark to your bed,' Clive added helpfully.

John was still glued to the television, so there was no chance of it being turned off any minute now. The bright fluorescent light above my head was burning my eyes and I remained under the covers in the hope that I might get some sleep.

Here I was, in an A-category prison, locked up in a cell with total strangers. I had noted while brushing my teeth that there was an alarm button just by the light switch but the notice beside it said: *You will be put on immediate report for improper use.* The alarm switch was very close to the light switch and I was informed later that inmates had often pressed the alarm while groping for the light in the night. I assumed my cellmates too were just as suspicious of me, not knowing my background or the reason I was in prison.

I had been allowed to keep my watch and I continued to look at the time, as I checked periodically to see whether there was any chance that John would be switching the lights and the TV off. It was two o'clock in the morning when the loud sound of snoring coming from John's direction suggested that he had fallen asleep while watching the TV. I raised my head and leaned over to look down at Clive, who was now also fast asleep.

The bunk bed creaked as I tried to descend the steps; this exercise proved more demanding than I had expected. The floor was miserably cold and I walked on it to the door, trying hard to negotiate my way in this tiny cramped space. I turned the light off, then the TV, and stood at the bottom of the steps wondering how I was going to get back up.

It was daunting, but I finally got to the top, got into bed and tried to fall asleep. Even at that late hour of the night there were sounds of music coming from other rooms and of guard dogs howling in the courtyards below. There was intermittent banging on the walls and a string of loud obscenities shouted from other cells. I do not believe I got more than an hour's sleep that night and, as the cell faced east and there were no curtains on the window, I found myself wide awake as the rising sun streaked through the window.

+ + +

An alarm bell rang at 7.15 a.m. It went off at the same time every day and once you heard it you were obliged to get out of bed, make the bed and get dressed. Dressing gowns and slippers were not allowed outside the cells, as I discovered later. I got out of bed and clambered down the steps to the floor. John had switched on the light and was at the sink. Clive had turned on the TV and was on the toilet. He was doing more than simply passing water or wind. The lingering smell, reminiscent of an operating theatre where a piece of bowel had been opened, was testimony to that. The gargling noise from the sink went on for over five minutes as I made my bed. I marvelled at how I had managed not to fall out of bed that night considering how narrow it was, but then I had not had much sleep.

After another five minutes Clive swapped places with John and I took the opportunity to get dressed. I changed from the tracksuit top and bottom I had been given into the spare set and decided that the other would serve for night-wear. I had not had a shower for twenty-four hours and was feeling sticky and uncomfortable. There was no shower in the cell and I was not sure what the arrangements were for washing other than at the single sink we all shared. The only shoes I had were the pair I came in but I was told by the inmates they were not appropriate for prison wear. Anyone found wearing nice outside shoes or clothes was going to be a target for bullying. I should get myself a pair of trainers, but there were no suggestions as to how I could acquire them.

'You have till eight a.m. to get ready in case you want to exercise and then have to go to work today,' John said. 'I've been here nearly four weeks and I still have no idea what happens from one day to the next.'

This last remark did nothing to boost my confidence.

'When the alarm bell goes off, you get up, do your toilet routine, get dressed and make your bed. Some screws come in to check that the bed is made and the cell is clean, or else trouble. You know what I mean? Also you have breakfast if you want any,' Clive advised.

I was beginning to get an idea what he meant.

I was the last to go to the toilet and when I got out the window was as wide open as the bars across it would allow, to help dissipate the smell. By now the stench was not just from the toilet – the food that had been left in the bucket underneath the sink was beginning to decompose. It was early November and having an open window was also letting in the cold. I washed my hands and brushed my teeth, walking around gingerly to avoid colliding with John and Clive. I had a bowl of Weetabix from my starter pack and there was enough hot water in the kettle for a cup of coffee. It was clear early on that I had a lot to learn.

+ + +

Just before eight there was the rattling of keys outside our cell. The cell door was opened, and the officer stepped in and shouted: 'Exercise?' He looked at each of us in turn and as I was the only one that took up his offer, he next spoke directly to me: 'In that case go now. You have about forty-five minutes.' I had been locked in this cell for the last thirteen hours and although it was a very cold morning, I welcomed the opportunity to get out. Exercise did not take place every day and only when there were enough officers to supervise, and it was not raining. I joined a long queue of inmates leaving the building waiting to be searched by two officers.

The exercise yard was a space the size of two tennis courts enclosed between two adjacent spurs and metal fences, topped by rolls and rolls of barbed wire. The whole area was covered by chicken wire to stop drugs and other illicit material from being thrown in from the street. There was grass in the middle bound by a paved path. There was no gym equipment and inmates were required to stroll around as many times as they could in the time allocated. For some inexplicable reason, everyone walked in an anticlockwise direction at varying speeds.

Those walking slowly in small groups chatted to their acquaintances while others took more brisk steps. Every now and again someone would stop as if to tie shoelaces and would surreptitiously pick something off the ground that had been dropped, always out of the sight of the officers. We were not allowed to stand near the buildings and were encouraged to keep walking. I saw a prisoner pass a small package to another prisoner in the courtyard during what appeared to be an innocent handshake.

I kept to myself but a couple of inmates stopped to say hello and introduce themselves. A bell was sounded after about forty-five minutes and we all drifted back to the entrance. We were all searched again on the way back in and I was back behind a locked cell door by 8.45 a.m. My cellmates were sitting on their beds watching breakfast TV. I was grateful to have had a brief spell outside, albeit in the cold.

+   +   +

The aim of the induction programme for inmates was to relay the routines, rules and expectations. We were given at least ten forms each to complete. A staff member came along and asked each participant if he was able to fill in the form or if he needed help. I was soon to discover that a significant number of inmates could not read or write. As the child of illiterate African parents, this shocked me.

The prison officer had a box containing over fifty small blue pens, each about five centimetres, barely long enough to be held comfortably for writing.

'Take one, and make sure you give it back at the end of the session,' the officer instructed.

I took a pen.

The prisoner next to me took a pen, rubbed the ball-point against the paper, muttered it was not working and proceeded to pick a second. When the staff member giving out the pens had his back to us, this prisoner winked at me and I saw him tuck the extra pen in his sock.

'They don't search your socks,' he leaned over and confided in me.

I was too new to the system and too cautious to want to be caught stealing a pen, much as I needed one.

'First we will talk about the telephone. This causes a good deal of confusion among inmates,' the inducting officer said, when he reached the section in the talk about communication.

He went on to explain that the first item on the canteen form (described later) was telephone credit. It came in units of £1 and each inmate could order as much credit as he wished, obviously within the allowance available to spend. Phone cards had long been dispensed with, as they were being used to buy drugs and perform other illicit dealings.

First we had to be allocated a phone personal identification number (PIN) and with a wry smile the officer pointed out that the system had been tightened so that phone credits could not be transferred to other users.

'You give us a list of the numbers you intend to call, together with the full details of the owner of each number: name, address and your relationship to the owner. We must be satisfied that the nominated recipient will want to receive phone calls from you. Then we vet them to make sure that they do not have criminal records.' The officer paused to make sure that we had taken in this information and went on: 'We must obviously also be certain that they are not victims of your crime.'

He continued: 'We do not want you to use these numbers to buy drugs from outside or to plan a prison breakout. You are allowed up to twenty phone numbers for family and friends and five for your lawyers.'

When a number was cleared it was linked to the PIN, so that the holder of that PIN could call only bona fide numbers. All phone calls were recorded and could be listened to.

Because of the limited numbers of phones, each phone call was programmed to last only ten minutes; each caller could not make another call for at least another twenty minutes. Phone calls could only be made during association, the time of day when we were allowed out of our cells and allowed to mix with other prisoners, which was approximately two hours each day. There were no phones in cells and the prison did not allow incoming calls to prisoners.

Mobile phones were forbidden. I discovered later talking to other inmates that the prison had several tools for detecting the presence and use of mobiles including searches of cells, use of inmates as informants and electronic detectors.

'You are allowed to write and receive as many letters as you like,' the officer advised. 'You can write to family, friends and your lawyers, and unlike phones, the addresses to which you write will not need to be vetted first. However, all letters coming into and out of prison will be read. I shall say more about letters a little later.'

+ + +

After lunch came the PowerPoint presentation about prisoners' behaviour and the different means available to impose discipline.

'One thing you will hear a lot about is the expression IEP,' the officer presenting informed us, as he pointed to the abbreviation on the slide. 'You can read more about it in your hand-out but it's one of the tools we have for punishing prisoners who do not obey the rules and those who cause trouble.'

We all looked keenly around the room to see if there was some object or device about to be introduced that would be used as a tool of punishment. 'Used properly it can also be a means to reward those of you who behave yourselves,' the officer continued. 'In the past every inmate moved up one notch in the prison pecking order once they had spent a certain amount of time inside, but under the IEP system you have to work for it.'

'What's IEP stand for, guv?' an inmate asked from back of the class.

'*Incentives and earned privileges,*' the officer went on.*
'I have to warn you we don't take any shit from any of you

---

* Incentives and earned privileges (IEP) was a system introduced
in prisons in 1995 with important changes announced by the
then Justice Secretary, Chris Grayling, in 2013. It was designed to
encourage good behaviour and performance and reduce reoffending
by prisoners by 'making [people in prison] work towards their
rehabilitation'. There were three levels of IEP: basic, standard and
enhanced. As of 1 November 2013, all prisoners coming into prison
for the first time were placed at a level between basic and standard,
referred to as 'entry' level. They were elevated to standard after
fourteen days if they behaved well. Progression to the enhanced
level was made more difficult under the new rules and was judged
to be through good behaviour and effort on the part of the inmate,
rather than merely from the absence of bad behaviour. At any point
the prisoner could be 'issued with an IEP', the local term for being
reported for poor behaviour or performance or breach of discipline,
and if found wanting can have their privilege status downgraded.

The IEP status governed a large number of allowances available to
prisoners, from being permitted to wear outside clothes, to having
televisions sets in their cells and even being granted approval to buy
additional items such as DVD players. These revised rules expressly
banned books from being sent in to prisoners. At Belmarsh (category
A) and Highpoint (category C) prisons, for example those on basic
status had the TV set removed from their cells and the number of social
visits they could receive was reduced. The salary for full-time work
was £5 a week for basic prisoners, £15 a week for standard and £25 a
week for enhanced prisoners doing exactly the same job. The prisoner
on basic entitlement had access to only £5 of any personal money in his
account per week, whereas for a standard prisoner it was £12.50 and
for an enhanced prisoner £25. This was an important point because
irrespective of the amount of money in the prisoner's private account,
he could spend only the amount dictated by his IEP status.

There was widespread concern that prison staff were abusing the
IEP system. This system was put in place not only to punish but also
to encourage good behaviour, but unfortunately it seemed to be used
more for the former. Throughout my stay in prison I saw numerous
negative IEPs issued, but never any positive ones.

I did cleaning jobs and helped inmates learn computer skills as a
peer mentor in education in Highpoint prison, and started cleaning
on first arriving at Hollesley Bay, but I was not rewarded with
enhanced status till after my induction in the latter prison.

in this place and if you cause any trouble, you will be issued with an IEP. This means there is a black mark against your name and if you get enough of these you will be called in front of the governor and you may pay dearly.'

He looked around to confirm he had our attention. 'Some privileges you have gained may be removed.'

+   +   +

'Your money will be available to you while you are in prison, but how it works will be explained to you on the wing,' the officer told me.

Money was the last thing on my mind, but I realised that soon I would need items such as stamps, which I would have to pay for from my own account.

Prisoners were not charged for food or lodgings; electricity, gas and water were free and there was no council tax levy. Materials for personal hygiene were also free and these included toothbrushes, toothpaste, soap, toilet rolls, body lotions, shaving gel, combs, hair gel and facecloths; and so were beddings and items for personal wear. Healthcare, including dental and eye care, were free at the point of delivery and there were no charges for transportation to and from hospital, when required. Inmates did not pay prescription charges and basic glasses, dentures and prostheses were offered free, as for the rest of the population.

What, then, did prisoners have to buy for themselves? Stamps, writing pads, envelopes and pens and pencils. That said, most prisoners helped themselves to pens from the education classes and from the reception rooms in their wings when they could get away with it. In closed prisons each prisoner was allowed to send one letter per week free of charge using specially provided writing paper and envelopes; the letters were sent second-class. Telephone calls were at the prisoners' own expense. Prisoners were allowed to cook in microwaves on some units but they had to buy their own ingredients, including a small selection of fresh vegetables, eggs, spices and cooking oil. There was a television set in every cell, except where this was temporarily withdrawn for disciplinary reasons, and the charge for TV use when I was in was £1 a week. Music systems, DVDs and CD players and radios were not provided. Those who smoked had to buy their own tobacco products and lighters.

There was no shop located in the prison. The canteen was a system devised that allowed inmates to mark on two sides of a sheet of A4 paper (the canteen form) the items they wished to buy and the prices charged. This was like a mail order scheme and the warehouse where they were processed was run by a commercial organisation and located outside the prison. One day a week a canteen form would be pushed under the cell door for each inmate. It would have at the top the prisoner's name, his IEP status (entry for me) and the amount available to spend (I had £14.33 to begin with in addition to the £120 I brought to prison with me). Below these were items that could be ordered.

Money, banknotes and coins, was forbidden. The temptation for inmates to steal money was therefore eliminated and the use of money to deal in drugs was reduced. Prison taught me that whatever obstacles man can invent, man can circumvent. Prisoners found other ways of selling and paying for drugs. For instance, canteen items could be exchanged for this purpose. My first haircut cost me a packet of biscuits. Drugs could be exchanged for other drugs of equivalent value (although I never worked out how inmates calculated how much cannabis to exchange for crack cocaine). Friends and relatives of a prisoner could pay a dealer; this surreptitious route for earning rewards was believed to be the way in which prison staff tempted to engage in this trade were paid. As with drugs, money could be smuggled into prison. I must admit I did not see banknotes but heard tales of prisoners with stashes of £50 notes in their cells.

Limiting how much money was available to the prisoner was one way of maintaining discipline. This way those with lots of money in their bank accounts outside could not use it directly to gain advantage or buy favouritism in prison, or at least the temptation and potential for this were controlled. There were tales of prisoners paying as much as £10,000 to prison staff for a mobile phone.

How did prisoners get income? Inmates were allowed as much money as they wished and this was paid into their private account. This was the same account into which the £120 I brought in was deposited. This could be topped up at any time by money paid in by family, and again there was no limit imposed as far as I was aware on the total amount that could be transferred. Catherine sent me a postal order for £100 the first time she sent me money.

The prison was more receptive to the idea of money coming from family members than from anyone else, in order to restrict drug money changing hands. Family were advised not to send cash, for fear of it going astray; cheques took up to ten days to clear and postal orders were preferred, as they were credited without delay. The post office, however, charged a hefty commission on postal orders.

The second source of income was money earned from engaging in work or in education and the salary paid depended on IEP status. As a prisoner on entry level pay during my first fourteen days in Belmarsh, for the number of times I was allowed out of the cell to work and to attend education classes, I would earn 50p an hour. The other income I would receive was £5 a week for being retired, and £1 of this was deducted for the TV in the cell.

By the end of induction, the grim reality of prison life was beginning to set in. Only one thing could be guaranteed and that was that I would be allowed out of the cell for two hours each day and during that time I would collect meals, have a shower and make phone calls if there was a phone available. Education (whatever that entailed), a library, workshops and gyms were available but there was no indication of whether or when I would have access to any of these. I could also apply to have visits from my family and lawyers, but the conditions were unclear. I should be prepared to be locked up in my cell for up to twenty-two hours each day.

Chapter Ten

A typical prison day would be as follows:

7.15	Bell rings to wake up
7.30	Prison officer comes round to do roll call
8.15	Exercise in yard if there are enough warders to supervise and it is not raining – forty-five minutes
9.00	Locked up in cell; rarely there would be an 'activity'
12.30	Collect lunch and bring back to eat in cell
13.30	Locked up in cell; rarely there would be an 'activity'
17.00	Association: meals, phone calls, shower, meeting other inmates
18.45	Locked up for the night

+ + +

The sound of a walkie-talkie got louder as the officer approached our cell door. We could hear the door of the next cell along being opened.

'Fuckin' screw on the corridor. I hope he opens the door to let us out,' said Clive.

The door was flung open. The officer stood with one foot inside.

'Miller, workshop,' he bellowed, as he stood aside to allow Clive out.

'What about me, guv, what am I doing this morning?' I said.

'Sorry, mate, I don't have you down for any activities today.'

'And me?' John said.

'You neither. Listen, I can only tell you what is on my list, and I do not make the fuckin' allocations.' The door slammed shut and was locked from the outside as John and I looked at each other in despair.

'This is meant to be a fuckin' working prison and everyone is meant to be allocated a job or a place in education,' John explained. 'Yet they only have places for less than a third of inmates at any one time. The rest spend the day locked up in their cells.' He sat on his bed, took off his trainers and then lay on top of his bed. 'Fuckin' waste of time,' he added, helpfully, 'and no wonder riots break out in prison.'

I did not know where to start preparing for a day locked in a cell. I had never before in my life faced, or been prepared for, such an occasion and could only liken it to being locked up in a toilet with two strangers and having to eat your meals and to sleep there.

I spent my time in silence writing letters to Catherine, Amy and Sophie. By this time I had been able to buy a pen and writing paper from the 'canteen'. I was keen to minimise the impact of what I was going through on them, so I spared them many of the details, but there was not much else to tell them. John read a book and listened to the TV. I had been warned during the induction programme that some inmates evaded questions about their backgrounds and about the crimes they were serving time for, or they would tell you in very vivid language to mind your own business. This reticence was perhaps understandable given that many of the inmates had never held a professional job, or any job they were proud of; I met one man who was determined to go back to being a drug courier. Being straight, he said, was too expensive. I discovered that many prisoners' families had fallen apart while they were inside and their friends had abandoned them.

John soon confided that he was sentenced to four years in prison for fraud but the trial had been a farce. He had been found guilty 'by association' but he would not elaborate. He was due to face a confiscation order and was worried that his wife and family would be thrown out of their home. He had been in Belmarsh for four weeks and was hoping to be transferred to a C-category prison soon.

John leaned over to the TV. 'There's supposed to be a fuckin' remote control but it was nicked last week,' he said, as he flicked through the channels manually. 'Channel one, *Homes Under the Hammer*; channel two, Attenborough documentary on monkeys and apes; channel three, *This Morning*; channel four, fuckin' advert; channel five, Jeremy Kyle, amazing the crap people get up to; channel six another fuckin' ad; channel seven, *Dinner Date*, fuckin' waste of time; channel eight, American soap, shit programme; channel nine, *Insanity*, cor, what a body and she has a lovely arse; channel ten, film channel, more repeats but occasional gems; channel eleven, prison radio; what a fuckin' waste of time. We get charged £1 each per week for all this crap.'

This routine was repeated at least a dozen times that morning.

'How do we go about getting our clothes washed?' I asked.

'Washdays on this wing are Wednesdays. Put all your dirty clothes in a string bag like this one and the laundry will do it for you.' He held a stretchable string bag the size of a carrier bag, 'but I suggest you do your underpants, socks, shirts or the like, there.' He pointed to the wash-basin on the wall.

'You mean the same sink we wash our hands in after we use the toilet, the same sink we wash our plates in after meals? The same sink we wash our faces in...?'

''Fraid so. That way you don't have to wait a week before you get them back.'

'But why shirts?'

'If you send them to the laundry they will come back a different colour. Everything gets washed together, whites, coloureds, the lot.'

We fell back into silence. I had often heard it said that one can be lonely in a crowd and the truth of this came home to me in my new surroundings. I missed my walk, my family and friends and most of all my freedom. On a day such as this I would be attending a Multidisciplinary Cancer Team meeting, doing a clinic, conducting a ward round, performing an operation or teaching. At the weekend I would be at home some of the time with my family and friends, being part of their lives. I was denied the simple things I had taken for granted in life. At home if I felt bored sitting in one room, I could easily walk to another for a change of scenery or go out. Here there was little alternative to sitting in the same place for hours and nothing could be more soul destroying.

By midday I had been confined to my cell for nearly nineteen hours, apart from forty-five minutes of reprieve to take exercise, with people I did not know, who might have been convicted of murder, firearm offences, bombings and grievous bodily harm. I was fearful for my safety but was powerless to change anything.

I had read about instances where inmates had attacked cellmates in prison. On one occasion in 2000 Zahid Mubarek, a nineteen-year old Asian prisoner, was beaten to death by a white inmate, Robert Stewart, aged twenty, in Feltham's young offenders' institution in London. During the inquest that followed it was revealed that prison wardens on duty knew of Stewart's racist and violent past and how he had written letters talking about his hatred for 'niggers' and 'Pakis'. It was alleged that staff were playing a game known as 'gladiator' or 'coliseum' in which unsuitable inmates were locked up together and bets taken to see how long it took before an assault took place. The practice, labelled a blood sport by the victim's solicitor, Imran Khan, was denied by the prison authorities.

+ + +

The tell-tale rattle of keys and footsteps returned at 11.50 a.m. when the cell door opened again, with the officer shouting: 'Dinner!'

John and I had prepared for this by making sure we were fully dressed and had shoes on. Clothing and footwear that were forbidden outside cells included vests, shorts, T-shirts, slippers and flip-flops. Failure to adhere to the strict dress code would result in the now well publicised IEP or report, or being sent back to, and locked up in, the cell. 'Middle Landing, far end,' he bellowed.

We picked up our plastic bowls and plates and headed to the line. Approximately two hundred inmates would now be served and I estimated that there were about fifty ahead of us. Many formed an orderly queue and took their places at the back, but a significant number jostled their way almost to the top, completely unchallenged. We hardly spoke to one another as we shuffled forward. There was an officer near the end of the landing at the gate and this was almost certainly the reason that there was some order in the way most inmates queued.

'Six at a time,' he instructed us we approached. He pointed to each inmate as they passed through the gate and said the count aloud. 'One, two, three, four, five, six –' and then held his palm out to the next in line, allowing about half a minute before letting the next batch through.

I was about ten people behind when he shouted: 'Next six!' The palm of his hand which was held up was lowered and waved towards the hotplate. 'One, two, three, four, five, six.' An inmate, who was seventh, barged on past the officer but was stopped. 'I said six, can't you fuckin' count? Get back and wait for your turn.'

When I got to the hotplate I waited in the queue that had just been allowed through. Three officers stood by the hotplate to ensure a well-ordered collection of food and prompt dispersal of inmates once the food was served. There was no social interaction at this time and I was commanded back to my cell. It was a strict policy in this prison that all meals were eaten in the cells. Once the three of us were inside with our meals, the big door was locked.

'Fuckin' waste of a morning,' Clive sighed as we sat down to eat. He had come straight from his morning activity, allowed into the cell to collect his dinner plate and bowl and commanded to the food queue. 'I spent the whole morning packing breakfast bags.'

'What did you have to do?' I asked.

'You have this big table, right? And there are bags with packets of cereals, another with sachets of sugar and another with sachets of powdered milk. Each packet of cereal had been made by filling a small plastic bag with enough breakfast for one person.' He paused to take a mouthful of his meal. 'You put one packet of cereal, five sachets of sugar and five sachets of milk together in a bigger plastic bag. You have this machine to seal the plastic bag and that is one breakfast pack. You do hundreds of those in the morning. Fuckin' repetitive, I was bored to death.'

'We all take it in turns to do the workshop,' John said. 'It'll probably be your turn next, David,' he continued. 'At least it gets you out of the cell. Also you get a chance to make a phone call on your PIN while you are out there.' I learned later that the privilege of making phone calls at that time of day was granted only to prisoners working in that particular workshop.

We finished eating, emptied the leftovers into the bucket under the sink and washed the plates in the basin. This was followed by cups of coffee and shortly after that the two others took off their shoes, lay on their beds and almost instantly fell asleep. I sat on the single chair and started to write another letter home.

+ + +

At about 1.30 p.m. John informed me to be ready to go out for education, workshop or gym, just in case I had been selected to participate. The selection process appeared to me to be random, and one, two or all three of us could be asked to proceed to activities. It was also possible that none of us would have any activity during that session. I sat on my bunk bed dressed in my prison tracksuit top and bottom and waited.

At just after 1.45 p.m. there was a sound on the corridor of jangling keys, footsteps and muffled instructions being given to inmates. The footsteps and the noise became muted, appeared to recede several doors away. The officer had walked past our cell and it was clear we had nothing to do that afternoon.

'Another fuckin' afternoon locked up in our cell,' Clive informed us.

The discomfort of spending the rest of the day locked up with not one but two strangers was almost palpable. During this time, we each moved as little as possible as there was almost no room for activity and we tried our best to keep out of one another's space. There was no meaningful conversation, as there was so little any of us wanted to talk about. There was of course a good deal that could have been said.

This pattern of confinement was repeated almost every day and the silence, the smell in the air, the sound from the television and the complete stripping away of personal freedom were painful and dehumanising. I must admit there were nights when I went to bed and hoped I would not wake up.

+ + +

At about 5 p.m. when the cell door was opened for what was referred to as 'association', I had been confined to the cell for twenty-three hours, except for forty-five minutes of exercise in the morning and about fifteen minutes to get my lunch.* Some inmates may not have been allowed out of their cells for exercise. In the short time that we were allowed out of our cells there was a lot to do. I wanted to talk to the officers to get information about what was in store for me over the coming days and weeks. As we had to queue for each of the activities, there was no prospect that much could be achieved. Pool and table tennis were the only two games for our use.

---

* Association was the coming together of inmates for social activities. The time allocated was also spent eating, playing games such as snooker, pool, cards and chess, and making phone calls, showering, doing paperwork and a host of other important tasks. It was an opportunity to leave the monotony of the cell. The time available for association depended on several factors, including prison category, prisoner's individual IEP status and the availability of staff. Prisoners classed as basic were not allowed out of their cells for association. When there was a shortage of prison officers the time was curtailed. It was approximately one hour and forty-five minutes a day in Belmarsh, three hours in Highpoint and practically the whole day in Hollesley Bay once planned activities were completed. Generally, inmates only encountered others from other wings during exercise, work and education as each wing was out of bounds to those who did not live in it. Association provided an opportunity to get to know other prisoners, make friends and seek advice from seasoned inmates. For some it was also a chance to sell, buy or exchange goods, but this trade was almost never legitimate.

There was a lot of chatter about high-profile prisoners. Asil Nadir, former CEO of the company Polly Peck, was held briefly in the same assembly room as me in Belmarsh prison and when he left almost all of the fifteen or so inmates had stories to tell about him.

Inmates from all backgrounds populated the prison and the stereotype of the average prisoner being male, black and young was a little misleading. Of course there were disproportionately more black people in prison than in the general population but this is not quite the same thing. There were doctors, lawyers, city workers, accountants, people from high positions in the press, entrepreneurs and even members of parliament and the judiciary. Looks can be deceptive and I learned never to judge an inmate's crime by his external appearance or demeanour.

This was the first time I saw the prison population from my spur in the same place at the same time. There was hardly room to move and everyone was trying their best to complete whatever task they had set for themselves in that limited time. Some inmates were prepared to use verbal intimidation or sheer muscle power to get what they wanted. I was told that some prisoners were already forming new gangs during this confinement and it was likely that they might confront opposing gangs. What was also noticeable and disturbing was how few members of staff there were. At an estimate, there could only have been five prison officers there, supervising the hundreds of prisoners. In this charged atmosphere, there was no doubt that this prison was overcrowded. Even more troubling was that there would be many more prisoners arriving this evening and I was unclear how many would be leaving to make room for the new arrivals, and where they would be sent.

I felt vulnerable and my anxieties were compounded by an almost complete lack of information from the officers. I had no idea what was happening to me from one day to the next. Many mornings and afternoons I had been ready to be let out of the cell for work or education only to be disappointed. I recalled my barrister telling me I would be in an A-category prison for only a few days and would be eligible to be transferred to an open prison in a short time. When I did eventually get the attention of an officer, discussions that took place were in full view and hearing of other prisoners; there was no privacy. Any requests about my day-to-day activities and my future location were met with the usual 'put in an app' response. Most so-called apps or applications that I submitted were either not acknowledged or those that were, were never acted upon. I was warned that making too many requests increased the risk of an inmate being regarded at best as a nuisance and at worst as a troublemaker, with serious consequences for one's chances of progression. My hopes were raised on a number of occasions when officers told me they would look into my requests only for me to be ignored by them when I came back hoping for answers.

People tended to congregate in groups during association. I had no time to play pool or table tennis and, besides, the prison's social hierarchy meant that only a select few ever made it to the games tables. By the time I had a shower, it was time to lock us up for the evening – 6.45 p.m. In the last twenty-four hours we had been, in prison speak, 'banged up' for nearly twenty-two hours. A tough night ahead.

The television provided much-needed distraction but there were no rules about which channels to watch. John left us in no doubt that he liked watching *Coronation Street* and *EastEnders* but Clive was happy just to have background sound and pictures. I preferred nature programmes, especially those presented by David Attenborough, which were mainly in the mornings. We all liked to keep up with the news, as newspapers were in short supply. Then a hand would appear, press buttons to flick through the channels and a different programme would be on.

I occupied my evenings writing letters and making extensive notes for this book. It was always painful replaying the memories of my incarceration and the dark times I was going through. As there was only one table and one chair between the three of us, we took it in turns to sit there when the other two inmates, too, needed to write letters or to fill in forms. At least they could sit on their beds and work, whereas I would have to do the difficult climb to the top of my bed, and it was not very convenient writing letters from such a height.

We took it in turns to use the toilet. I soon learned that a good way to reduce the smell was to flush the toilet as soon as you passed a stool, and to flush the toilet intermittently as soon as there was something in the bowl. Unfortunately my fellow inmates didn't pick up on this or could not be bothered. My profession, as a colorectal surgeon working with human excrement, had unexpected advantages: the smell did not bother me much. At least one person washed his undergarments each evening but clothes lines were not permitted, so we placed our washing on the large heating pipe that ran across the far end of the cell. In such a confined space, movement was kept to a minimum and I was surprised that more people did not get deep vein thromboses (DVTs). DVTs are more likely in people who are confined to small spaces and are not able to do much activity, such as in an aeroplane, hence they are also termed 'economy-class syndrome'.

We all watched the ten o'clock news together and it did not matter whether it was on BBC or ITV. One evening there was a news story about a prisoner who had absconded from a D-category prison. John sat up and said: 'I know that fucker. He was at Waylands with me when I was there three years ago. He can't afford to get out of prison because there is a drug gang waiting for him outside. If he sets foot on the outside they will kill him. He absconds regularly and the authorities always pick him up in the same place, his home. When they take him back he gets more time added to his sentence.'

Just how repetitive life was going to be began to dawn on me after that second night. We each used the toilet at about

11 p.m. and then went to brush our teeth before going to sleep. Another restless and noisy night loomed ahead. It was tedious getting into the top bed; I had to stand on the chair and climb the ladder, making sure I did not slip. As the whole structure shook and creaked each occupant stayed as still as possible. I made sure I had done all the chores I needed to do before I attempted the difficult climb, so I did not have to climb down once I was up there.

At my age I was grateful not to be afflicted by arthritis or lung disease. I spared a thought for the many inmates with physical disabilities in Victorian prisons with no lifts, long and narrow corridors and inaccessible accommodation on several floors. I had found an old library book at induction, which I now had with me in bed to read. I could only go to sleep when whoever was below me decided to turn the light out. Then I had to endure the restlessness of the occupant of the lower bunk, who caused the whole bed to shake every time he changed position in bed. He also snored, which John found so unbearable that sometimes he slept with his head next to the TV, which was left on all night.

I was woken up at 3 a.m. when the bed shook. The ceiling light was out but the TV was still on, and both of my cellmates were fast asleep. I got up, clambered down, turned the TV off and climbed back to bed. Neither of my cellmates stirred. Just as I fell asleep, the loud barking of a dog woke me up.

Chapter Eleven

To survive in prison, I needed credit for the phone to call my family, writing paper, pen and envelopes. I went one morning for education induction (paid £1.50) and one afternoon for work (£1.50). The total amount earned was added to money taken from my private account (£5 entry level IEP allowance – from the £120 I brought into prison) and my retired allowance of £5 pounds, less 33p for TV. This total, the so-called spending money, was all I was allowed to use that week, including phone calls. I was not able to make any phone calls (apart from the free call on my first evening) before Wednesday of the following week, eight days after my incarceration.

I ordered £10 for phone credit and four first-class stamps, a writing pad, a pen and a pack of envelopes. I have shown the amounts in some detail to dispel the myth frequently perpetuated in newspapers that prisoners are allowed so much money that they live in luxury when inside.

My stamps, writing pad and envelopes were delivered in a sealed transparent bag on the second Friday, day ten of my imprisonment, and on day eleven a new canteen form was delivered to repeat the process. The goods and receipt were sealed inside and were visible without opening the bag. This allowed the purchaser to check that the items bought were the right ones and the correct price had been charged. This was the pattern that was to recur throughout my stay at Belmarsh – canteen forms on Saturdays and the goods ordered delivered the following Friday, and there were no facilities to purchase any items outside of this arrangement. This system was the same in all the prisons I was moved to, although the canteen days varied. Clearly it was important to order thoughtfully to make sure I had all I needed during the week and to use what I had frugally to ensure it did not run out before the next canteen.

Items on the canteen list were chosen by the governor from a national list and were selected to meet important standards:

Health and safety and security: the goods should not be of such a quality that they could be used as weapons; most liquid items were supplied in plastic rather than glass bottles. It was interesting to note however that pilchards and vegetables such as spinach were supplied in metal tins, but the tin opener was made of plastic and there were no rules about the disposal of the opened tin or the lid.

Decency: indecent material was not allowed.

Appropriateness: alcohol was forbidden and there were materials for religious use such as rosary beads and Muslim caps (or Taqiyahs, the only other headgear permitted in prison). Sikh prisoners were permitted to continue wearing turbans.

Tobacco and lighters were permitted but the irony that the latter could be used to set fire to the prison was lost on the authorities.

Everyone looked forward to the days when canteen items were delivered, as these few additional items made life a little easier. I particularly liked bananas but there was a problem. I bought a bunch of them in Highpoint but they all ripened at the same time and I had to eat them all in one day.

Day 8, Wednesday, Belmarsh

Typically, on Wednesdays, in my former life I would be in the operating theatre all day at Ealing Hospital doing major bowel procedures. Instead here I was in prison. For breakfast I had muesli and made coffee with the semi-skimmed UHT milk. I watched the morning news programme. John was called for a gym session at 8.40 a.m., so Clive and I were left to complain about another morning locked up in a cold cell. It was raining, which was why our exercise had been cancelled.

I had been to the library and obtained, among the six books I was allowed, Jeffrey Archer's novel *Not a Penny More, Not a Penny Less*. I was engrossed in an account of a surgeon who had been conned into making an investment in an oil company and lost his money. To recoup exactly how much he was owed he set up an elaborate plot in which he followed the perpetrator to another country and induced an attack of gallbladder pain in him by spiking his drink. The surgeon then proceeded to do an operation on his victim by making a superficial incision on his tummy and stitching him up again. The surgeon had obtained a large gallstone from the museum in a London teaching hospital, which he used to convince his victim that he had had his gallbladder removed. The patient was charged exactly the amount of money that he had extracted from the surgeon in the initial con. I wondered how this surgeon would have fared in front of the regulatory body, the GMC, if he had been called upon to explain these exploits.

At about 9.30 a.m. the huge cell door flung open and the officer who stepped in held a card in front of him and said, 'Sal-oo?' with the emphasis on the second syllable.

'Yes, guv.' I held up my hand.

'Pack all your things, you are moving out. You have ten minutes.'

'Where am I going...?'

The door slammed shut.

No response.

'Where do you think I might be going?' I asked Clive.

'You've only been here a week, so I do not think you are moving to another prison,' Clive calculated. 'More likely another cell. They will often tell you not to pack bed linen, et cetera if you are going to another prison. Each prison supplies its own bed linen.'

'But why would they want to move me to another cell?' I asked, irritated, as I began to grab my belongings and shove them into the clear prison-issued plastic bags.

'Many inmates believe this is a form of punishment. Also if they suspect there is drug-taking in the cell they split the inmates up. The other reason is to provide space for new prisoners. There are people coming in every day.'

I put papers and books first in one bag; then my plastic crockery and cutlery; the remains of my canteen starter pack comprising tea, coffee, a packet of biscuits, and milk; toothbrush, toothpaste, soap; each time lifting the whole bag to make sure it was not too heavy. Bedding, towel, shoes, prison-issued jogging top and bottom in another bag. I finished stuffing all my effects into three bags, which I placed in the middle of the room. It was going to be a struggle carrying these three bags, especially if I had to climb stairs.

'You've obviously not been here long enough,' Clive commented. 'It's easier if you tie two bags together like this.' He went on to make two ends out of the top of one bag and tie them to the corresponding ends of the second bag. 'This way you can carry the two bags over one shoulder. If you do the knot the way I have, the bags don't come apart as you lug them.' He was describing a reef knot, unaware that as a surgeon I had tied it many hundreds of thousands of times in my career. This knot is a secure way of stitching tissues and tying off the cut ends of blood vessels and is used scores of times by surgeons in a single operation.

Another officer opened the cell door, came inside, looked sternly at me and said, 'Are you Sell-you?'

Before I could answer, he said, 'Follow me.'

'Where am I going?' I asked, as I placed the two bags strung together over my right shoulder and picked up the single bag with my left.

'Up the stairs, top floor, last room on the right.'

I staggered to the top floor and waited by the cell door. The label on the door had one name and I felt relieved. The officer now opened the door just wide enough to get me inside, slammed it loudly and locked it behind him.

+ + +

I was surprised to find the only occupant lying on the top bunk of the double bed. I went straight for the single bed and I deposited my bags on the floor next to it before looking up at my new cellmate. He was a black man with short hair and he can't have been older than twenty-two years. He was dressed in prison tracksuit top and bottom and had a thick jumper over his top.

'I'm David,' I introduced myself.

'Hi,' he said reluctantly as he turned away to watch the television, which was on at high volume.

'What's your name?' I probed, as it would be helpful to be able to address him by his first name.

The label outside gave his initial.

'Nathan,' he said, almost as if he was speaking to the television.

I decided to unpack only the items I needed day-to-day, and keep the rest in the bag. I had no idea when I would be moved. I tried hard to strike up a conversation with Nathan but he was not giving much away. At least John and Clive spoke when spoken to and would indicate when there were questions they weren't going to reply to. Reluctantly Nathan admitted after much probing that he had been arrested while on a short trip from Jamaica to visit his sister. It was an uncomfortable feeling sharing a cell with someone who was unwilling to communicate. He was probably younger than my youngest son, he was in a foreign jail and he looked depressed.

I would have liked to offer help but he clearly wanted to be left alone, which I respected. I was looking for someone to be a mentor to, but what experience did I have to share with him? Mentoring takes many forms in prison. A mentor could be someone with a lot of inside knowledge of the prison system who could informally advise others about procedures and on how to get around the administrative obstacles. It could be someone who merely listened to others pour out their grief as a form of relief for them. There were also trained mentors giving formal advice on numerous issues such as drug rehabilitation. A mentor I encountered later in Belmarsh prison, who had been sentenced to over twenty-five years behind bars, was put in the position where he had to support another inmate who could not cope with a two-year sentence.

But on what moral authority could I give advice to Nathan about how to lead a life without crime, when I was a criminal myself? One of the difficulties I was beginning to experience was adapting to this constantly changing social landscape and not knowing where I fitted into it.

There were times when I feared for my physical safety. I envisaged it would be very easy for me to be overpowered by someone much younger and more athletic, whose history I knew nothing about. The cursory screening test I had gone through to determine my risk of harming others and myself did not give me much confidence. The alarm bell was unlikely to be much use in an emergency, and it was located where it could not be easily reached and any would-be assailant could block access to it as part of an attack strategy. Somehow I'd felt safer when I was with two other people in the cell than I did being alone with one other stranger. I imagined this was probably a mutual feeling, but Nathan did not show any outward sign of discomfort about being alone with me.

On the positive side, there was only one person with whom to share our limited space. Nathan had only one bag of possessions and most were still in the bag. What was out was neatly arranged in the space he had chosen for himself, and he was clean.

At lunchtime, Nathan stayed in his bed when the door was opened and I sensed that he probably wanted to join the queue without me next to him. When I brought my lunch back he was not there but joined about five minutes later. The cell door was locked and we ate without saying a word to each other; the only sound was from the television. Nathan allowed me to wash my plastic crockery and cutlery first and as soon as he finished washing his he jumped back on top of his bed.

+ + +

It was a relief to be out of the cell for a session in education that afternoon. The subject was drug education and about twelve prisoners attended. Everyone seemed to know more about drugs than I did. I'd already come across the smell of cannabis but knew better than to report this to an officer. I realised that the consequences of *grassing* (an old pun) on others could be serious. A common occurrence was the sound of inmates shouting out of their windows through-out the night. They were referred to in prison as 'window warriors' and such individuals were probably suffering from drug or alcohol withdrawal. There were units dedi-cated to the care of inmates suffering from substance abuse, but I never got to see these specialised blocks. A number of inmates on the general units were using opioid substitutes such as methadone and buprenorphine. Healthcare staff delivered these medications daily. There were notices on the boards advertising the various preventive and management interventions for drug users. A number of inmates I spoke to would have liked a more robust programme for long-term rehabilitation from drug use beyond the handing out of substitutes.

Alcoholics Anonymous, a self-help organisation set up to assist those in the population who are committed to recover from alcoholism, held regular meetings. Later on, I would take the opportunity of attending one of these informal gatherings and would recommend them to anyone with alco-hol-related problems. Right now, I found myself sitting in a semicircle in the small room with a projector showing Power-Point slides. The door was locked and there was a guard outside minding several classes. The paradox of this was probably lost on the prison authorities, but if one or more inmates attacked a member of staff, it would be too late for anyone outside to come to their rescue. All the female staff I encountered wore trousers and I was told the reason was to reduce the risk of sexual attacks. Although they gave the impression of being confident and able to protect themselves in the event of an attack, I wondered how staff, especially women, felt in this environment.

A register was kept and only one person was allowed to go to the toilet at any one time. For once in my adult life I had to ask permission to be allowed to go to the toilet and even when permission was granted, I had to wait till the inmate before me, who had the toilet pass, returned. The blood pressure tablets I was taking increased the amount of urine I passed each day, so I had to make sure that I asked for authorisation to go to the toilet long before I needed to. The young teacher who led the discussion was confident and knowledgeable and she discouraged private talk between inmates. There was therefore little opportunity for social interactions other than through the class. Inmates exchanged greetings and brief pleasantries on the long corridors, touching fists, doing high fives or gentle embraces.

I was pleased to see Nathan, whom I had met only a few hours earlier. I explained to him what I had done that afternoon, but he did not seem interested and all I got out of him about what he had done that afternoon was a disinterested 'not much'. Much as I tried, there was little conversation or interaction between us for the whole of the evening and he went to bed early, leaving it to me to turn the TV off and the light out. Neither seemed to bother him as he slept.

+ + +

Neither of us had any activities the next day and we spent most of the early morning in silence. At about 11 a.m. the cell door was opened by an officer and in walked a tall white man in his mid-thirties wearing a smart Nike tracksuit top and bottom and with smart Adidas trainers. He sported a two-day growth on his face and had very short blond hair. He deposited the three bags he was carrying as the cell door was locked, held his right hand out to me and said:

'Hi, I'm Richard.'

'Hi, I'm David,' I said as I shook hands. He looked over the top of the bunk bed and did the same to Nathan. Nathan hardly took his eyes off the television and slowly extended his hand for a limp handshake.

'Nathan,' he said, took his hand away and continued to watch the box.

'Fuckin' place has not changed since I was last here,' Richard complained. 'The food is crap, the screws are fuckers, the place is overcrowded and you are treated like a piece of shit.'

'Second time back in Belmarsh, back to hell?' I said.

'Third,' he corrected, 'not counting the five other prisons I've been in.' He looked at Nathan and asked: 'Are you sure you want to stay on the top bed? Most people choose to sleep on the lower bunk, and as you were here before me, you get the first choice.'

'I'm OK.'

Here was someone who appeared to know his way round. He untied his bags and in no time at all I saw the most immaculately made bed. 'If you manage to get an extra bed sheet, place it under the mattress,' he advised.

'What good will that do?' I enquired, bemused.

'You should have noticed by now that not long into the night all your bed sheets are off the top of the bed. The reason is the fuckin' sheets are too small. You tie the ends of the sheet under the mattress to the corresponding ends of the top sheet on top of the mattress, or better still to the blanket.'

'What a good idea,' I acknowledged. 'But where do you get spare sheets from? They only give out two, one to go on top of the mattress and the other over you when you lie down'

'Easy. Sheets are often left lying around, and you just pinch one when you get a chance.'

'OK. By the way, we do not have a plug in the washbasin,' I said, 'it's gone, someone must have nicked it.'

'No problem with that,' came the reply. 'Put two or three used teabags in the small plastic bag that your cereal came in, tie off the end and just plonk it in the plug hole.'

Richard continued to remove things from his plastic bags and noted: 'Normally that shelf and part of the other one belong to the bottom bed,' as he pointed to the wall. 'I hope you don't mind if I rearrange things.'

'Please go ahead,' I said. Nathan said nothing.

Ten minutes later the shelves were neatly stacked. Without any prompting, Richard was prepared to lay bare his prison history. 'Third time I have been done for drugs. First two times I was supplying them on the streets but the money was too slow coming in. So I decided to be a courier and to bring them in from abroad.'

I was surprised by his candour.

'Which countries?' I asked.

'West Africa mainly. Nigeria and Ghana mostly. This last time I was caught coming from Ghana. I found it expensive going straight but my girlfriend had a baby a few weeks ago. When I get out I don't think I will be coming this way again.'

I was surprised that he had not asked where I came from.

+ + +

None of us had any allocated activity outside of the cell that afternoon. For the rest of the day Richard and I chatted while Nathan remained largely silent. Richard was a mine of advice about prison life and I found his tips extremely helpful.

'You will have noticed that the water is not very warm when you have a shower. The trick is not to press the push button all the way in. Just halfway. I figured that the hot water came first from the mixer tap, and then the cold water. Pressing some of the way allows more hot water than cold water, do you see?' as he did a demonstration with his right thumb.

I saw that someone like Richard would be a helpful source of information for many of the issues I was struggling with, such as how to expedite my movements to an open prison. The prison officers I had managed to talk to so far had been far from helpful. Richard suggested that I was more likely to go to a C-category prison before being transferred to an open prison and he proved to be right later.

After much persistent interrogation from him I told Richard I was a doctor.

'I guessed as much. I can suss you guys from miles away,' he said confidently.

'How can you tell?'

'You look like one. You speak like one. Educated accent. You wash your hands after you've had a crap, innit? You take notes every day and your writing is fuckin' terrible.'

'Well, thanks very much, but my writing is not that bad.'

'Piece of advice from me,' Richard went on. 'Don't let on in prison that you are a quack. If others find out, they will bully you till you have nowhere to hide. They fink every doctor in prison went to the Harold Shipman School of Medicine. Professional killers, know what I mean?'

I did not tell Richard *why* I was in prison. He assumed that I was in for fraud for fiddling my practice expenses. When he was last in prison, he'd met a senior hospital doctor who had claimed huge amounts of money for duties he did not do and when the authorities finally figured out what he had been doing they reported him to the police. Richard assumed that financial swindling also was common among doctors. I was grateful for his advice. I was definitely going to keep my medical background to myself.

Chapter Twelve

Personal visits were the most important dates in my empty calendar, especially in those grim early days of my incarceration. There was nothing that I looked forward to more than seeing my wife and children and perhaps the occasional friend. The information I received on how to arrange visits was patchy and I supplemented this by talking to inmates and some reluctant members of staff.

My IEP status on first imprisonment was *entry* but was raised to *standard* by the time I applied to have visitors; as such it allowed me three social visits per month. This would be increased to four if I were elevated to *enhanced*. I was also entitled to a visit by my legal team. Visitors would not be permitted merely to turn up unannounced and I had to decide beforehand who could visit. There were three main reasons for this that I could work out. First, potential visitors had to be vetted to reduce the risk of contraband, especially drugs and weapons, being smuggled into prison. Any visitor caught smuggling drugs into prison was liable to criminal prosecution. Second, it attempted to obviate the possibility of perpetrators of crime coming face-to-face with their victims. I heard an account of a victim trying to come to prison to take revenge on the prisoner who was serving time for stabbing him during an argument a year or so earlier.

Third, also for the prisoner's own protection, it was important that only those he chose were able to visit him. The prison obviously wanted to avoid revenge attacks on prisoners, but some inmates exploited this arrangement to nurture their infidelities. I witnessed an occasion where a prisoner was visited by a female partner and four children on one visit and two weeks later by a different partner and a new set of three children, who also addressed him as Daddy.

A maximum of three adults was allowed per visit but three additional people under the age of eighteen could visit at the same time. This obviously posed problems for our family, with my wife and four adult children. Add to that list my brother and brothers-in-law and their families and it meant they had to take turns visiting me.

I had to submit a visiting order (VO) for each visit and for each person nominated I had to provide a full name, date of birth and age, address, contact telephone number and my relationship to that person. Each visitor had to provide two items of identification, one of which had to have a picture – a passport or driving licence – and the second of which could be a utility bill, or a bank statement for visitors coming from abroad. Visitors were searched. Sniffer dogs were on site. All possessions, including handbags, wallets and watches, were placed in lockers. A limited amount of money carried in transparent bags was allowed, to buy tea, coffee and snacks in the snack bar run by the prison.

The dress code for visitors was not widely advertised but attire that was considered sexually provocative was prohibited. It had been known for inmates to spend a lot of the visiting time engaging in intimate touching under short dresses, even under the watchful eyes of the prison guards.

Two weeks after I arrived at Belmarsh, my name appeared on a board. The following day my cell door was opened just after 1 p.m.

'Sellu, visit!' the officer shouted.

All prisoners going for visits had to wear standard attire issued by the prison. At Belmarsh it was a burgundy tracksuit top and bottom and a pair of trainers. My family were not allowed to send me trainers so I was issued with an old pair with worn soles. (I did not have enough money on my canteen to buy myself new trainers.) The last time my family had seen me was when I was led away to the cells in the Old Bailey in a work suit. Here in prison I was just another anonymous prisoner. I was not allowed to take anything to the visiting hall, not even a piece of paper or pen that would have helped to prepare my thoughts for the visit or to take notes during the visit.

The officer pointed to the assembly area where I was comprehensively searched and then sent to a waiting room. There were about nine inmates uttering expletives to describe the state of the prisons, the conditions they were held in and the attitudes of the officers. About forty minutes later the door was opened by an officer, my name called and after a series of doors were unlocked, some ten centimetres thick, we reached the final holding area. It was a good half an hour before the door opened and we were summoned one by one, with our names ticked off a list.

'I see you have your fuckin' watch on. Were you not told it is not allowed on a visit?'

'No, I did not know, or I would have left it behind in the cell,' I told the prison officer.

'Take it off, we will hold on to it, but in future don't bring it on a visit.'

I walked through an X-ray detector which beeped as it picked up the metal buckle of my belt.

I had to wear a belt or the prison-issue jogging bottoms, which were two sizes too big for me, would fall off. I must admit I felt like an idiot wearing a belt over tracksuit bottoms, but in prison one had to make do with what one was given. I was now given a bright yellow tabard to wear over my top. This was one of the ways prisoners were distinguished from visitors.

The visitors' hall was slightly bigger than a basketball court. As I walked through the door there was a stage to my right and on it sat officers with a board that had all our names and the seating arrangement. There were several rows extending from right to left and each had numbered positions, about two paces from the next. At each position there were four seats arranged around a rectangular table and the prisoner sat on the chair that was a different colour from the other three and faced the officers who were guarding the hall.

There were large posters displayed prominently on the walls spelling out the rules in the visiting hall: visitors must be modestly dressed and the only touching allowed was a hug on first contact and one at the end of the visit. Intimate contacts between prisoners and visitors were strictly prohibited. Prisoners were to remain seated throughout and if anyone left to go to the toilet they would be searched fully on return. Only visitors were allowed to go to the snack bar, which was located to the far left on the same side as the officers' stage. There were staff patrolling the whole floor and there was also CCTV in operation at all times and anyone caught contravening the rules would be barred from receiving further visits, or worse. If drugs were involved, those caught would be arrested and prosecuted and imprisoned, if convicted.

Catherine had come with James and Sophie, our daughter. James had come especially from Manchester two days earlier. They said I had visibly lost weight. Without a decent mirror and with an old disposable razor I had also shaved badly that morning, and I was told I had not managed to make it clean.

This was the first time I was seeing my family since I had been taken away unceremoniously at the Old Bailey some two weeks earlier. We had spoken on the phone and exchanged letters but this was the first face-to-face contact. We hugged and wept and for several minutes we remained silent.

'How are you?' Catherine was the first to find words but even these were uttered between sobs.

When we finally recovered, we did our best to catch up with events since my imprisonment. Catherine, James, Sophie, Denis (my brother) and Tom (my brother-in-law) had gone to see my lawyers the day after I was sent to prison and they discussed the trial, my conviction and the sentence. They were told there was no prospect of an appeal and I should be prepared to accept that I would have to serve my sentence. However they reiterated that they were assured I would serve less than half of this sentence behind bars, as 'prison authorities are uncomfortable having someone of his status on their hands'. They were told moreover that I would be transferred to an open prison within two or three weeks of my incarceration and would spend the rest of my sentence there.

My family were appalled at the conditions I had described in prison but knew there was nothing I or they could do to change things.

I enquired about everyone's well-being and about their jobs. James had finished his intercalated Master's degree in medical research, which he had passed with merit, and was now studying in earnest for his final medical examinations.

He, like everyone else, was deeply traumatised by my suffering during the previous three and a half years, the trial and my prison sentence. No one was eating or sleeping well and they all spent most of their evenings in a darkened house worrying about the conditions in which I was held.

There were also practical matters to do with money. I had not worked for several months but still had to continue paying our mortgage from our savings. There were issues with my pension, which Catherine was discussing with the director of finance at Ealing Hospital and with my financial adviser. I had earned a comfortable salary doing private practice, but my salary had been stopped abruptly.

How was Daniel, our son in Muscat? How was Amy, our eldest daughter? There were many more questions but I was not really able to absorb all the answers. We had coffee and I had my first drink of Diet Coke since being locked up. The one hour and forty-five minutes we spent together passed very quickly and it was soon time for us to part. Part of the two hours dedicated for visiting had been used up by some of the time it took for us undergo the check-in process. The lights were switched on and off several times and then came the announcement telling us time was up and would all visitors get up and make an orderly exit. At first there was no response, so the announcement was repeated three minutes later, this time in a more authoritative tone. Hugs again and like the initial meeting the breakup of the visit was hugely emotional.

I put my glasses on and watched as Catherine, James and Sophie went out through the exit. After a final wave I sat down, as instructed, and looked down at the floor as the last of the visitors made their way out. The officer instructed us each to clear our tables and throw what was on them in the bin at the door as we went out, but in the meantime to remain seated.

I did not eat much that evening and went to bed early, telling my cellmates that the visit had gone well.

+ + +

I had a visit from the detectives who had conducted my case to take fingerprints and DNA samples from me. I was informed this was routine for all prisoners.

'We will hold these samples in our database,' the detective said aggressively. 'If you have ever engaged in any sort of crime or do so after this, we will be able to identify you from these samples. If you have nicked a Mars Bar and left your fingerprint at the site we can pick it up once these samples are processed.'

'I can assure you I am not a criminal and have never engaged in criminal activity,' I said, knowing full well that my definition of criminal was at variance to theirs.

Why else would I be locked up in here?

+ + +

There were difficulties and frustrations with the telephone system. It wasn't uncommon to have to queue for up to forty minutes, only to be told to return to your cell because association time had expired or it was meal time just when you had reached the front of the queue. There were a number of ploys to get around having to queue; one common one was for inmates to stand in the queue for a few minutes, turn around to the person behind them and ask them to reserve the place so he could go to the toilet. This was often an excuse to go and do something else such as have a smoke, but officers outlawed this practice.

I witnessed an occasion where an inmate, let's call him Fred, came from almost nowhere to the phone as soon as it was available, ignoring the long line of people who had been waiting to use it. The inmate Joe, whose rightful turn it was, understandably protested, as he had been waiting in the queue for half an hour.

'It's my turn to use the phone,' exclaimed Fred, as he grabbed the handset. 'Ah was in line b'fore you. I had to go and collect me washing.'

'No, it's my fuckin' turn, you stupid ass,' shouted Joe, encouraged by others in the line. 'Ad've seen you if you was in the queue. Anyhow, if even you were, that's not allowed.'

'Who the fuck are yer to tell me what is allowed in a prison and what's not?'

Tempers were beginning to rise as the shouting got louder, and a fight was likely to ensue. There were no officers to be seen.

'You good for nothing murderer, you mother fucker.'

'Well, look who's talking! The pot calling the kettle black. You're in for murder, too, shithole.'

'Yea, but my situation is different. You stabbed your fuckin' victim in the back. At least my victim had the flammin' chance to put up a fight and defend himself. I knocked him cold with one blow.'

'I will kill you if you don't get off out of my bloody way.'

This was a threat to be taken seriously. After a few further exchanges an officer came on the scene, interrupting what was about to develop into something serious. He ordered the two to their respective cells.

Even among murderers it seemed some forms of killing were more abhorrent than others.

+   +   +

Iftikhar was in his forties. I shared a spur with him. He was training to be a solicitor when he hit on the idea of arranging sham weddings, which was a money earner. He realised he could not do this on his own and had to work in a gang comprising a solicitor, a registrar of marriages and a priest. His role was to 'groom' the prospective brides first by arranging their trips from various parts of Europe. They had to be able to speak a reasonable amount of English and of course had to be the right ages for their matches. Most of the grooms were men already in the UK who wanted to get citizenship by marrying someone who was legally a European citizen.

Having learned about the groom in detail, Iftikhar would not only recount this to the bride but would spend the day acting the part of the man and testing the bride on various aspects of his life. Where was he born? What was his job? How did they meet? Where did they plan to live when they married? Names and background information on in-laws, and so on. He would find out as much about the bride as possible and similarly recounted her history to the groom, who rehearsed the same exercise.

Next the prospective partners would spend a day together with Iftikhar and he would coach them as a pair and take pictures of them posing as a happy courting couple. The weddings took place in a registry office they had infiltrated or in a particular church with a bent pastor, and they all made 'good money'. The bride was paid off at the end of each wedding and went her way; the groom, at whose expense this was carried out, would soon be the proud owner of a residence permit that would entitle him subsequently to apply for a British passport.

That was until the authorities intervened. This particular group had come to their attention some time before and they were rounded up during a wedding ceremony; they were each given jail sentences ranging from five to seven years and any assets the authorities could get their hands on were confiscated.

+ + +

Olu was of Nigerian origin but a naturalised British citizen. In his late thirties, he was a member of a small but 'highly organised' (his words) group, some of them based in Nigeria. The scam for extorting money was well known and came in various forms. The group got hold of the email addresses, phone numbers and postal addresses of people who appeared to be wealthy and vulnerable, and would bombard them with implausible tales with promises of big money for the victim.

Only two years earlier I had received an email telling me that my grandfather had died in the 9/11 disaster. He had owned a goldmine in Senegal and had over £50 million in a bank in Dakar. This particular group said they had tried to trace all relatives and I was the only person they felt they could do business with, but I was not sure how they came to that conclusion. The money had to be claimed within a certain period, at the end of which the bank would confiscate any funds not disbursed. The email made it clear that I was not to reply to the message if I was going to be a time waster or was looking to engage in dishonest deals. However, if I was seriously interested, I was to send a reply with my bank details, which would be verified as authentic before such a huge sum could be transferred to it. However, there were upfront fees that I had to pay to cover their administrative costs.

Olu told me they used other ploys. Some victims would be told of large wins in lotteries they had not taken part in; some were chosen clearly at random for large sums left by altruistic donors in their wills; or money had been left in a storage building and they were looking for someone to help them launder it for a large reward.

'Surely nobody falls for such obvious plots,' I challenged him.

'You'd be surprised how many gullible people there are out there,' was his reply.

Once a victim started to take the bait, money was demanded from them as an administrative fee to begin the transaction. If the victim paid money, more and more demands followed until several thousand pounds had been obtained. Shockingly, in one case a lady paid nearly £100,000. There were even instances where potential victims were flown to Nigeria and a reception laid on to give an air of authenticity to proceedings. They were met at the airport by 'officials' dressed in what appeared to be genuine government apparel and were driven in cars with official-looking colours and number plates.

The gang was intercepted when a suspicious individual reported them to the police and the members were caught. Long prison sentences were imposed and their assets confiscated.

'We lost our home and my wife is now living with our children in the home of one of her relatives,' he said morosely.

Chapter Thirteen

Day 28, 8 a.m.

An officer opened the door of the cell:

'Sellu?'

'Yes, officer.'

'You have ten minutes, pack your things. You are moving.'

'But where to?'

He ignored this question.

'No need to pack your bed linen. Someone will be back soon to collect you.'

As he locked the cell door and disappeared, I looked at Richard, whom I could always rely on for clues.

'Prisoners are never told when they are being transferred to other prisons. They think you will inform your pals outside and they might ambush the prison van along the way,' Richard said wisely.

All manner of thoughts were racing through my mind. By now I had become accustomed to putting all my belongings into large plastic bags and tying them together, so I could carry them with less difficulty than before. If I were going to be moved to another prison, would it be an open prison or not? Richard did not think so, as it was unusual to transfer to an open prison from an A-category prison such as Belmarsh. It was more common to send inmates first to a C-category (closed) prison. I would not be allowed to use the phone at this time of day, so there was no way of informing my family if I was going to be moved out. I did not even know where I was going, but I hoped it would not be to yet another cell in Belmarsh.

+ + +

I sat in the waiting room in Belmarsh, awaiting transport to HMP Highpoint South. I had no idea where Highpoint was but anywhere was preferable to *Hellmarsh*. These had been the worst twenty-eight days of my life.

The waiting room was about five steps by five and had a bench along the wall. The door was locked and in common with other rooms in prison there were thick bars across the windows. There were about seven people in the room and I gathered from the animated conversation that we were all moving to other prisons.

The bespectacled Asian man sitting next to me turned around to look at me and I said hello to him. He looked in his early sixties and I still remember his warm smile and clean-shaven, youthful face.

'I'm David,' I said, happy to see a friendly face.

'I'm Samir,' he replied.

'Are you waiting to go to Highpoint?'

'Yes,' he replied 'and I hope we leave soon. What about you?'

'Yes, me too. It will be nice to get out of this hellhole.'

'I agree.'

We continued to talk, exchanging information about our experience, each of us careful not to give away much about our convictions. He had been incarcerated in September 2013 and like me he had been moved a number of times within Belmarsh and had shared cells throughout, some of the time with some high-profile prisoners. This was also his first time in prison and never again, he vowed.

'Are you from London?' he asked.

'Hillingdon, just outside West London.'

'What a coincidence. I live in Southall, just off the A40.' His eyes lit up.

We discovered that our homes were about twenty minutes' drive apart. He owned a business in West London and when he asked me where I had worked I told him the truth: Ealing Hospital.

'That's my local hospital, and I must tell you I have seen you there before. I thought your face looked familiar.'

Two inmates were pacing up and down and one kicked the door, indicating his desire to go to the toilet. It was fifteen minutes before an officer came to let him out.

'I have been told that most cells in Highpoint are shared. If we have to share can we put our names down to share a cell?' he asked.

'Great idea,' I said, pleased at the opportunity to be in the same cell with someone I got on with. 'I don't smoke.'

'Neither do I,' he assured me.

+ + +

Any enthusiasm about leaving Belmarsh was tempered on entering the sweatbox. The faster the vehicle travelled the more uncomfortable the ride became, aggravating the feeling of nausea. First I shut my eyes, then I concentrated hard to look outside to ease my discomfort. On the positive side, each new prison meant I was making slow progress towards my final discharge. At this stage I had a slightly better idea of the routines I was likely to expect at the other end.

It was a relief to arrive, and get out, nearly two hours later.

+ + +

'You must not kick the fuckin' door, and whoever does so next will get an IEP,' said the officer with a stern countenance.

We were in a waiting room with a dozen inmates and the atmosphere was becoming increasingly tense. Every few minutes an inmate would kick the door, hard, to signal his request to go to the toilet. Samir, sitting next to me, looked over and shook his head. There were no-smoking notices in big letters on the wall, but this did not stop several inmates lighting up their rolls of tobacco. None of the officers who came in mentioned the thick clouds of smoke.

I was not sure what system was being used to determine the order in which the names were selected, but inmates who had arrived after us were being called out first. Just before 5 p.m., Samir's name was called out. We had agreed that whoever got out first should enquire about our wish to share a cell.

It was not till 7 p.m., five hours after we arrived, that I was summoned.

I found out that Dilip, an inmate who was working as an orderly, was conducting the reception and interview. He was in his forties, stockily built and had a small moustache. It was his duty to welcome each new prisoner, collect data from him on matters such as religion, race, smoking, dietary preferences and other issues relating to needs. Dilip also gave information about prison procedures, rules and generally how to stay in the good books of the officers.

'Keep your head down,' he advised. 'You will find that things are more relaxed here compared to Belmarsh.'

When we met and I told Dilip my name, he informed me that an inmate named Samir, whom he had interviewed earlier and who had been taken to the induction block, had asked if we could be placed in the same cell, and was this OK by me? I said it was and he promised he would do his best to make sure we were lodged together.

Once these checks were over about half a dozen of us placed our bags on a large trolley, which I helped push, and we made our way to the induction wing. It was divided into two spurs, G and H. G was the induction spur and H the enhanced. My bags were offloaded outside the reception office and I was instructed to collect my meal from the hotplate. The meal, the vegetarian option, had been standing in an unheated room and was very cold by now. Holding it in one hand, I took two bags over my other shoulder. Dilip kindly helped to carry my third bag and confirmed that I was sharing a cell with Samir.

The new cell had clearly been designed for a single occupant. The room was five steps long and the fixtures were the bunk bed to the left, toilet basin and sink to the right just by the door and a desk and chair by the window at the far end, with a shelf above it. There was very little floor space. The cell was extremely cold; the windows had gaping gaps, which Samir had stuffed with toilet paper. There was no curtain.

Samir had arrived three hours earlier and had worked tirelessly to clean the cell and arrange his affairs. He had taken the bottom bed and hoped that was all right by me, as he had trouble with one knee and it would be difficult for him to do the climb. I did not mind. He had left space on the shelf and also on the table drawer for my things, which was very thoughtful.

A few bed sheets previous inmates had sewn together enclosed the toilet bowl on the floor and the cistern above it, and while they offered a modicum of privacy, did nothing to disguise the smell. Opening the window was a poor option, owing to the miserable weather outside, but there was no other means of ventilation.

'Eat your meal and I will help you unpack, if you want,' Samir offered.

I took one bite of the pasta, and could only manage another three mouthfuls, before emptying the leftovers into the bin beneath the sink.

'These are awful and inhumane conditions, Samir, but we have to be strong to see this through. Let us not allow the system to break us.' For the first time I had found a cellmate who had a temperament similar to mine and whom I could talk to and to whom I could offer support.

'We have our families who are there for us and I agree we must stay strong. Things are going to be difficult.' Samir had been in Belmarsh two months earlier and I could imagine that he had gone through far worse than I had.

He was due to be released in March 2014, in just over three months' time.

I unpacked only essential items, as Dilip had told me we would be in induction for a week or two and would then be transferred to a longer-term unit. We talked about our families and how they too had been humiliated by the events that brought us here and by our incarceration.

Keen to get some sleep, I crawled into my bunk with books sent by Jonathan Aitken when I was in Belmarsh, *Prayers for People under Pressure* and *Psalms for People under Pressure*. The former Conservative Member of

Parliament and cabinet minister had been found guilty of perjury in 1999 and sentenced to eighteen months, of which he served seven behind bars. After his sentence he went to Oxford to study Christian theology. I was full of admiration for the clarity and style of his writing. I had no idea how he found me or knew about me, but would find out much later that we had a mutual friend, Steve Morris, an Anglican priest who used to visit Ealing Hospital.

There was the small problem of turning the light out at night and, as had been the case at Belmarsh, I could not reach the light switch from my bunk and I would have to climb down a ladder to turn the light out. Samir said he wanted to have an early night, but he would get up once I had finished reading to switch the light off. All I had to do was let him know.

It must have been midnight when I finally decided to go to sleep. I slid down the ladder as quietly as I could, passed urine and flushed the powerful toilet and switched the light off. The noise was deafening and in the darkness Samir said: 'I told you to wake me up to turn the light off.'

'Well, I was going for a pee, so I had to get up anyway. Good night.'

Samir was up at about six and was moving about stealthily, undoubtedly to avoid waking me up. But the bed was so creaky that as soon as he got out of it, I woke up.

'Good morning. Can I make you some tea? I have my own teabags and the tea tastes better than the stuff the prison supplies.'

'That's very kind of you, but not just yet. I will have some later, thanks.'

'I hope you don't mind me using the toilet. I can't wait to go and it will be at least two and a half hours before our cell door is opened. Smelly, I'm afraid.'

'Can't be helped, Samir,' I assured him.

I was glad that I was sharing space with someone who, like me, was prepared to show consideration and respect for a cellmate.

The cell door was opened at 8.20 a.m. and we were both keen to get out on the corridor to stretch our legs and have a small change of scenery, although we now discovered that we were free to wander only within the building, on the landings and in the little hall outside the cells. We agreed that one of us should always stay in the cell, as items such as plugs in the sink, the remote control for the TV, cartons of milk, sugar, coffee, stamps and writing paper were targets for thieves.

+ + +

We had a new routine.

8.30: cell doors opened and those who had managed to sign up for work or education were allowed out of the building till lunchtime. Those who were not in employment remained in their cells or could wander within the building. 12.15: We convened for lunch, which we would be required to have in our cells. Work and education were from 13.40, supper at 5 and association until 18.45, when cell doors were locked. Unlike at Belmarsh, where the activity each prisoner was allowed was allocated on a day-to-day basis, at Highpoint, the onus was on the inmate to find work or sign up for education. As places on these programmes were severely limited the prospects of a place on them were poor. Reasons for wanting placement were that the weekly wages were higher for those engaged in activities and they were more likely to have their IEP status upgraded to the enhanced category.

We were handed forms on which to apply for placement; it took eight weeks before I was accepted as a classroom assistant, teaching computer applications to other inmates. In the meantime, I took the opportunity to use the gymnasium for some sorely needed exercise.

We were given information on the prison's policy towards family contact, as summarised by the Prisons Handbook, 2012. 'Establishments will operate policies and practices which enable prisoners to exercise the right to communicate with bodies outside the prison, in particular to ensure the maintenance of their family ties. In doing so they will ensure that proper restrictions are in place to maintain security, good order and discipline, to prevent crime, and to protect the interests of victims and the general public.'

Books and puzzles were not allowed to be sent in by post and registered mail was banned. My daughter Amy placed an order with Amazon to send me an Arabic textbook, which she paid for. The book was delivered to Highpoint Prison but I was not allowed to receive it and so it was placed with my possessions, to be handed to me on final release from prison. As I needed this book for my studies, Amy bought another copy and photocopied five or so pages at a time and sent them to me by post. Bizarrely, these were permitted. It took over ten weeks to get the whole book to me as photocopies and the postage alone was several times the cost of the book. This incomprehensible and perverse ban on books from outside was lifted in 2015.

+ + +

During opening hours we met up with a few fellow inmates from Belmarsh and had the opportunity to exchange stories about our encounters so far, and our prospects.

'The officers here are more polite but are not very helpful,' I was frequently told. 'If you pester them too much, you stand out as a troublemaker and that can affect your prospects of moving to a nice unit.' Food for thought. 'Some units here are crapholes.' I was told that units nine and ten were good, six and seven were Portakabins but were OK, but some of the rest were to be avoided if there was a choice. They were dirty, noisy, drug-infested and housed dangerous inmates. We had no choice.

After we had been at association a handful of times, Samir came back to tell me that he had met a few inmates working as orderlies who could 'pull strings' with the officers to help us move to a nice unit, get good jobs or enter the education classes of our choice. He also informed me that he had just seen an inmate cutting hair and coincidentally this barber was a friend of an inmate Samir had shared cells with in Belmarsh prison. Samir had spoken to the barber and asked if he could cut my hair. I had told Samir that I had not had a haircut in months and this was obvious to him from the nature of my bushy hair and the time it took me to comb it during the day. The barber had said he would but wanted me to go immediately and could I take 'something' with me as a fee. I asked Samir what he would suggest and he said a packet of biscuits, which we had. I put a packet of biscuits in my pocket and went to the hall where there was a small group of people gathered around an inmate who was cutting another's hair.

I made my way through the group and introduced myself to the barber:

'Hi. I am David and Samir says you have kindly agreed to cut my hair.'

He looked up at me, said hello and told me he would cut my hair after the person on the chair.

I was surprised that he had a reasonable set of barbering tools including a pair of clippers, scissors and a mirror, but I did not see any razors. I picked up a mirror and when I took a look at myself, I was horrified by the sight of my shrunken face staring out of my bushy hair. My face was gaunt; I was only partially shaven, with clusters of hairs on my chin. I had not had the opportunity to have a haircut in several weeks.

My barber suggested a short haircut, as there was no guarantee I would find someone else to cut my hair in the coming months. When he finished he remarked, flatteringly, that I looked handsome. I gave him the packet of biscuits and helped sweep up the hair.

+ + +

Samir and I queued together to collect our meals – our cell was always within sight when we stood in line. Later we went to the gym together. We coordinated our shower times so that one of us went first while the other remained in the cell. We agreed on which TV programmes to watch. We both liked nature programmes, snooker and the news. Samir was keen on the soaps, especially *EastEnders,* during which I would read my emails and letters, write my diary and reply to mail. I liked quiz programmes such as *Mastermind* and *University Challenge.* I knew very few of the answers, but perhaps the pleasure was in seeing someone else sweating under questioning (and losing the contest rather than landing a prison sentence). I enjoyed documentaries and while I watched them Samir did some reading. He was a staunch Hindu and read religious scriptures avidly. I often continued to read and write when Samir went to bed but I did so by the light of the TV tuned to the radio station, which had a static screen with light that was not particularly bright.

We also did our best to provide mutual psychological support. Each evening we would discuss our unfortunate fate but would exhort each other to remain strong and to call on all our resources to see our sentences through.

The identical spur on the other side of reception was the enhanced wing or Unit H, which was out of bounds to induction inmates. All the cells there were single except for the last four. These were double cells, each twice the size of our current cell with, we were told, its own separate toilet. Samir and I decided that we would like to share the double cell on the H spur, if at all possible. We were not sure what criteria were used to determine who was given which units, and as the officers did not discuss this with us there were rumours of favouritism. Inmates also complained that officers who wanted to punish them for minor misdemeanours sent them to what they labelled *crap units*. It appeared that officers used the sanction as a means of imposing discipline on prisoners.

Chapter Fourteen

One evening Samir announced that he had spoken to one of the orderlies who promised he would have a word with a senior officer to ask if we could be moved together to a double room. Our prayers were answered when a couple of days later we were moved to the cell we wanted. Cell H14 was twice the size of our single cell. The toilet was housed in a separate room, though the door had been removed and replaced with a sheet of tarpaulin-like fabric; the cell was much warmer than any other room in the building, we were informed, and there were two beds on opposite walls.

We dropped our bags and did a high five.

The window looked into the same bleak courtyard from the far side of the building, but it had curtains made out of two bath towels; they were crude but did make a difference in keeping out the morning light.

We continued our same routines; going out for exercise in the courtyard together, applying for the same courses in education and pooling most of our supplies, such as soap, new razors, shampoo, biscuits, milk, tea, coffee and fruit collected from the servery.

I remember one evening vividly. One of us always had the strength to cheer the other through a difficult day but on this particular day we were both struggling emotionally. There was no specific trigger, only that we missed our families and our lives. Staff shortages, which meant we were banged up for longer than normal, did not help. Each time the cell door was shut, it was not simply pulled closed, it was slammed as loudly as can be imagined and the noise was uncomfortable in volume, almost like an explosion. This was an act that generated enormous stress and got our heartbeats racing. We went through the whole evening not saying a single word to each other except a good night at bedtime.

Later, we spoke about this evening often to try to understand its significance. We were not ignoring each other, but were running short of the mental strength needed to comfort each other on a difficult day. We were both mature enough to recognise that no offence was intended and we knew each other well enough to realise that at such times it was best to remain silent.

The next day was much better. We went to the gym together.

+ + +

Highpoint, at that time, held over thirteen hundred inmates. The gym was open seven days a week from 8.15 a.m. to 7.15 p.m. and had room for about sixty inmates at any one time. As most exercise sessions lasted about an hour it was clearly necessary to allocate sessions to enable fair access for all inmates. I had applied at induction to be allowed to use the gym, careful not to admit that I was being treated with medications for high blood pressure. There were always cries of dissatisfaction when gym sessions were cancelled owing to staff shortages or other unforeseen incidents. I attended the gym at least three times a week.

There were posters on the walls with different messages.

'You did not take pills to help you get fat, why do you need them to help you slim?'

'The only time you cannot exercise is when you are dead, so stop making excuses.'

'Bollocks to cancer,' explaining how to do testicular self-examination and what abnormalities to look for.

Groups of inmates huddled around these posters, reading the messages. There was high praise for the equipment and the helpfulness of the gym staff at Highpoint. For someone who did very little exercise at home due to a gruelling workload this was a valuable way to spend time. The exercise helped to relieve some of the enormous stress I suffered along with feelings of anger and frustration. The time in the gym was also an opportunity to get out of my cell. Indeed, many inmates came to the gym mainly for this reason and engaged in very little activity, other than a gentle stroll around the rackets court.

It is clear from the foregoing that prisoners attending the gym were a captive audience, and the gym could therefore be used to promote messages about drug and substance abuse, about cancer awareness, the value of a healthy diet and other important issues. One session a month could be devoted to showing films and DVDs or holding discussion groups, and continuing use of gym facilities could depend on compulsory attendance for at least one session every three months.

+ + +

'Which of you is Pathak?'

The cell door swung open.

'Me,' Samir answered.

'Get up now, get ready and come out in five minutes. You have been selected to have an MDT.'

Before anyone could ask any questions the officer was gone.

'What is an MDT?' Samir asked me.

'I think it is drug testing, mandatory drug testing.'

I had read up about this in the packs that we were given when we first came to this prison.

'You have nothing to worry about,' I said, believing he was not into drugs from what I had learned about him.

When he came back some two hours later he brought a piece of paper telling him his test was negative. He was allowed to leave once his test result was known but three of the inmates who were with him were ordered to stay. Presumably they tested positive.

A report showing a negative result was important, for it showed that at the time of testing the prisoner could prove he had not been taking any drugs, and this would count in a parole hearing. If the sample tested positive the prisoner could arrange an independent analysis at his expense. The prison authorities were obliged to allow this test before prescribing any punishment against the inmate. It was a disciplinary offence for a prisoner to refuse to participate in an MDT. Prisoners who wished to be helped to kick the drug habit could submit to a voluntary test and a positive result in such cases would not be subject to disciplinary action.

Dealing in drugs was big business. The dealer in prison, if he could get away with it, could earn plenty of material items and privileges from other inmates. I heard of a dealer who had his room cleaned, and his bed made daily, his clothes washed and ironed, and his hair cut by those prisoners he supplied, as well as being able to acquire extra goods from the canteen. He allegedly had an illicit mobile phone, which was charged for him three times weekly. Mobile phones presumably got into the prison through the same routes as other items such as drugs.

The first time I was exposed to cannabis was when I was a trainee casualty officer at Ancoats Hospital in Manchester in 1974. A patient or visitor had smoked the drug in the department and a more senior doctor brought me into the room and asked me to take note of the smell. It was a distinctive smell that I never forgot. I had noted this smell on patients' clothing over the years and many I confronted admitted to having smoked the drug.

I wondered how drugs could be smuggled into such a high security jail as Belmarsh but, as is well known, prisoners are infinitely inventive; they devise new techniques to circumvent whatever restrictions are in place. Many prisoners I spoke to were convinced that prison staff were involved in smuggling drugs into prison. I understand that civilian prison staff such as teachers, librarians and cooks were searched but even these searches were cursory and they were allowed to bring in food items, which could easily be used to hide drugs. According to prison rules, 'An officer shall submit himself to be searched in the prison if governor so directs. Any such search shall be conducted in as seemly a manner as is consistent with discovering anything concealed.' This implies that prison officers were not routinely searched and only at the discretion of the governor. It was also claimed that a more comprehensive programme of searching would be so time-consuming that it would interfere with the smooth running of the prison and antagonise staff.

My IEP status remained standard, meaning I could have only three visits per month. Catherine told me many of my colleagues, including Ian Franklin, a consultant vascular surgeon, had asked if they could come and see me there, but with so few visiting opportunities, we decided to restrict visitors to family members only.

Prisoners were required to wear prison-issued striped white and blue shirts, blue jeans and trainers but nothing else, even on a cold day. To get to the visitors' hall we had to wait at an outside gate (in the cold and rain) for about twenty minutes before an officer would let us through to the hall. We then queued, partly outside, to get to the reception desk, where we were individually checked, thoroughly searched, put through a scanner and then told to go into the hall.

Groups of visitors could not be split up; there was no facility for confidential one-on-ones. As a family we had no secrets from one another but it would have meant a great deal to me to have been able to talk to Catherine alone. We established a routine in which we went through topics: I asked about the children not present at the visit, about my brother Denis and his family, about my brothers-in-law Tom and Tony and their families and about nieces and nephews. Then we would discuss colleagues who had been so supportive, especially Ian Franklin and Simon Payne. Matters then moved to the events at home, press coverage of my case (of which there was a lot, and which was mostly derogatory about me), financial matters including the mortgage on the house, insurance policies, my pension, Catherine's work, bearing in mind the stress she was going through, the allotment at home (largely abandoned during the winter) and other practical issues.

We tended to defer discussions relating to life inside prison till later in the visit. I often tended to downplay what I was going through but the long pauses between words, my attempts to hold back tears and looking at the ground as I spoke, gave away my feelings. For someone who had spent his days making life-and-death decisions, imprisonment was not easy. Then came my wife's words of support and reassurance: *keep strong; keep your chin up; you have nothing to be ashamed of; you have helped so many people and saved so many lives*.

Catherine would give me news of the website set up by my dear friend and staunch supporter Ian Franklin and the messages of support started pouring in. I was always pleased to hear of the warm and enthusiastic words from patients, colleagues and friends. These messages were printed and sent to me by mail, but I was glad to hear them summarised. There were delegations by Catherine and some of her friends to Members of Parliament to bring their attention to my plight and to see if I could be moved to an open prison.

The act of parting was never less than heart-wrenching; each goodbye was as painful as the last. I would watch my family leave without me and the weight of the sentence we were all forced to serve would come crashing back down on me, like a great weight.

+ + +

Over the coming weeks Samir and I discussed getting together when we were discharged from prison and arranging family meetings and meals together. His leaving date was at the beginning of March and he promised to visit my family when he got home. I was going to remain in prison for almost eleven months after he left and as I did not know anyone else as well as I did Samir, I decided that I would apply to move to a single cell once he was gone.

In the meantime, my family, friends and colleagues were lobbying hard to expedite my transfer to an open prison. Two of our workmates visited their MPs at the beginning of the year asking them to look into what they reported was a miscarriage of justice in my case. A large body of doctors in Ealing Hospital wrote a letter to the Minister of Justice asking for my case to be reviewed and in the meantime for me to be moved to an open prison.

I had an unexpected visit from the deputy governor. A man in his early fifties, smartly dressed in a suit and glasses, he introduced himself in his office, where I now sat, and told me he had received a letter from the Ministry of Justice about my case. He promised to investigate my case in the light of the new information they had; if he came to any different conclusion about my case he would be in touch. He said he made no promises, gave no details and did not entertain any questions. The meeting lasted about five minutes.

The following morning, on the way back from the gym, I was informed by a female officer: 'Mr Sellu, the deputy governor has instructed us to transfer you to Unit 10. Go and pack and you will be moved as soon as we have an officer free to take you over there.'

I had not been addressed as *Mister* in prison until now.

Samir and I looked at each other.

'Will I be going into a single cell?' I enquired.

'I believe so, but I'm not sure.'

Given the choice, I would have preferred to stay where I was, with my friend, but given that Samir would be leaving to go home in six weeks and I would either have to move or be forced to share the cell with someone I did not know, moving now into a single cell was preferable to staying put.

Samir helped me pack. We shared equitably all our collective items and he carried two of my bags for me to reception.

Several inmates coming back to the unit muttered: 'Are the twins moving out?'

The officer approached: 'The orderly is here with the trolley. Time to go.'

'Am I allowed to come with David to Unit 10, to help with his bags?' said Samir.

'No, not allowed.'

'I will keep in touch,' said Samir.

'Look after yourself and keep strong.' We embraced and I left without looking back.

I wrote to Samir once before he left in March. Prison rules forbade me to contact him through the internal post and so I had to use the external post. I told him how much being together had meant to me and thanked him for all the support he had offered. Our friendship had made an unpleasant experience just that little bit more tolerable.

+ + +

Unit 10 was a modern block that housed older prisoners and those serving long life sentences. My bags were deposited outside the duty staff office and I waited in the corridor until an officer was free. The cell I was allocated to was near the far end on the ground floor and it measured the usual five steps by three. The officer, to my surprise, now handed me a key and said it was for me to use to allow myself into and out of my cell. Unlike the induction block, I was now allowed to wander out of my cell and into the courtyard at any time during the day as long as I stayed within the perimeter fence around the unit. I was keen to take advantage of this new, unexpected freedom whenever I had the opportunity. (We were locked in at night and were confined to the cell till the doors were opened again in the morning. Freedom depended on there being enough prison officers on duty to supervise inmates getting out of their cells. There would be occasions when, owing to staff shortages, we were confined to our rooms for up to twenty-two hours a day.)

The windows had curtains. I even had my own shower and toilet in a small but separate room attached to the cell. Now that I had my own space, I used the opportunity to continue to write about my experiences in prison.

Chapter Fifteen

A little over three months after arriving at Highpoint Prison, I noticed that my feet were swollen; the left side was more swollen than the right. When I pressed with my finger it left a dent on the swollen part – this physical sign is referred to as 'pitting oedema'. I had been to the gym four times that week and thought that maybe I had overdone things. When I woke up on Sunday, there was just a little hint of swelling but by tea time, it had recurred and extended to the middle of my calf on the left and just above my ankle on the right. The left leg ached a little, probably from being heavier than normal, but I had no pain. I was walking one and a half miles on the treadmill and cycling six miles on the exercise bike in the gym without any pain and with just the expected shortness of breath. This was considerably more exercise than I'd taken at home. I had experienced no pains in my chest and I was not coughing up blood.

There are several reasons why legs swell. Leg swelling is a recognised side effect of Amlodipine, the blood pressure-lowering medication I was taking. I might have damaged the muscles in my calves from the sustained bouts of exercise, or I might have been on my feet longer than I was accustomed to. Being locked up several hours a day in a cell takes away any incentive to be active and encouraged prolonged periods of sitting still in one place. While the gym was a good place to exercise, it was in relatively short bursts and there were still long periods of inactivity for the rest of the day.

One serious cause of swelling of the legs is deep vein thrombosis (DVT). One danger of DVT is that the clot that forms in the vein can break up and migrate to the heart and then into the lungs where it can block a major (pulmonary) artery supplying the lungs. This is known as a pulmonary embolus, or PE, which can be fatal. Another complication of a DVT is damage to the valves in the veins that direct blood to flow from the legs to the heart. If the valves cannot function, the legs become permanently swollen and the tissues above the ankle can break down, resulting in venous ulcers that are difficult to heal.

Just before tea I went to the unit office and tried to explain my concern to the prison officer sitting behind the desk. 'I am particularly worried because one side is more swollen than the other, and that makes it important to rule out a DVT,' I explained.

The officer looked away from the computer, briefly at my exposed legs and then at me, and said, 'Put in an app.'

'But that will take ages to process,' I protested.

'Tell them what you just told me and mark it *urgent*.'

That was Sunday evening. On my way back to the cell I took a self-referral form from the pile next to the healthcare postbox, completed it with all the relevant information and underlined the words:

I am concerned I have a DVT.

I made a duplicate copy of this form and took one copy back to the collection box, as I was required to.

As I had heard nothing by Friday that week, a full five days after I first complained and filled in the referral form, I went to the office in the morning and complained to another officer. I also pointed out that we were coming to another weekend and there was even less likelihood anything would be done till Monday.

The officer picked up the phone, dialled the healthcare centre and after explaining what I had told him he said, reassuringly, 'He knows what he is talking about because he has a medical background and he is not one to make trivial complaints.'

When he put the phone down he turned to me to explain: the health centre ran an on-call system on Fridays and over the weekend, so there would be no doctor there that afternoon. In any case, for all problems, inmates would first see a nurse who would do a triage assessment and then decide whether the inmate would see a doctor or not. If it was deemed necessary to consult a doctor the nurse decided how quickly this would happen. I would be allowed to go and see the nurse at 2 p.m. and I was instructed to come down just before when there would be an officer to accompany me and other prisoners to the health centre.

I had been to the health centre twice before. The waiting area stank of tobacco despite the no-smoking sign on the wall. Two inmates got out their roll-up cigarettes, lit them and started smoking. One said to the other, after he counted the number of people in the room: 'Twelve people here this afternoon, fuckin' two and a half hours before everyone is seen and we can go back.'

The waiting room was a good place to get snippets of news from other units. 'Two fuckers on Unit Six had a punch-up this morning. Summat to do with one grassing on the other about a mobile phone,' one of the two smokers said to the other, loud enough for everyone to hear.

+ + +

A woman in nurses' scrubs opened the door to the waiting room. She had a large bunch of keys on the end of the chain attached to a belt round her middle and the uniform was ill fitting. She called out a name (no Mister this time) and an inmate got up and walked towards the door. She said nothing to the smokers and I supposed this was in the hope that someone else would tackle them.

As we waited, the complaints about the healthcare service, doctors and nurses were becoming louder. The doctors were alleged to be insensitive, the nurses looked down upon prisoners, and the service was demeaning, the other prisoners said. They were given no dignity and respect even when they had genuine medical problems.

One and a half hours after we arrived in the waiting room, the door opened and the man I presumed was an orderly stood at the door and shouted 'Sellu!' I answered, got up and followed him down the narrow corridor. He stopped to lock the door behind him after fumbling for some time to get the correct key from the large bunch he was wearing and then pointed to a door marked 'Dr' further along.

A dapper middle-aged gentleman with a large frame invited me to sit on the chair on the other side of the table, sat down and said: 'I am Dr H.'

'David Sellu,' I replied, as I laid my glasses on the table.

Dr H looked at the computer: 'You are not on my list.'

He got up, opened the door and said to the man who had shown me in: 'For the nurse, not for me.'

I got up, rolled up both legs of the prison tracksuit bottoms I was wearing and showed him my calves. 'As you can see, both my legs are swollen, but the left is bigger. I am concerned I may have a DVT. I am a doctor.'

Dr H gestured towards the door, making it clear that he was not going to see me.

'With all respect,' I protested, 'I need to see a doctor.'

'The nurse will see you,' he said firmly. I rolled down my tracksuit bottoms, picked up my glasses and returned to the waiting room.

'That was quick,' an inmate remarked.

'I am afraid the doctor would not see me and has passed me over to the nurse,' I explained.

'You should have punched him in the fuckin' nose.'

There were murmurs of dissatisfaction and looks of disappointment, mercifully not directed at me, and it was another twenty minutes before I was called again.

Three doors were opened and unlocked. The nurse did not introduce herself. I told her my history and rolled the legs of my jogging bottoms up again as I spoke.

'I am a doctor,' I said as I concluded, 'and I am worried that I may have a DVT.'

'Have you been struck off by your medical regulator yet?' she asked coldly.

I was sickened by her lack of professionalism. I had imagined that those in the medical field who chose to work in prisons had the same level of compassion as those elsewhere in the health service.

'Are you going to examine my legs or get someone else to see me?' I said.

She looked at my legs, prodded the left calf in two places and concluded that I might have a DVT. She asked the orderly to lock me up in a different waiting room next to her room.

'What are you going to do?' I asked as I exited her room.

'I will let the doctor know.'

I stood just outside the door: 'What's your name?'

'Sarah.'

I waited yet another thirty minutes before the officer who had brought us from the units opened the door. Behind him was Nurse Sarah.

'You can go back to your unit now,' she said.

'What are you going to do about my legs?' I wasn't giving up, as she was about to walk away. 'Is the doctor going to see me?'

Nurse Sarah looked at the officer, then turned to me and said: 'I am going to refer you to A&E.'

I discovered later that prisoners were not allowed to have any advance warning of appointments outside prison. This was apparently a precaution the authorities took to prevent prisoners from arranging for someone outside to hijack the vehicle and free them.

I was told to go to my cell and change into my prison clothes, the same ones we wore when we made contact with any members of the public: a short-sleeved shirt with narrow white and blue stripes, and jeans.

+ + +

I was told by the officer whose job it was to escort me that he was taking me to the West Suffolk A&E Department. Having treated prisoners at Ealing Hospital, I recalled that they almost always came handcuffed to prison officers, something I regarded as humiliating. On those occasions the officers had told me that this was as much for my protection as it was for security.

'Will I be handcuffed?' I asked, anxiously.

'Oh, yes,' he said cheerfully. 'Throughout the journey, both ways.'

Fifteen minutes later the officer returned carrying a bag and was followed by another slightly older colleague with blonde cropped hair. He had a folder on the front of which was a grainy picture of me taken when I first arrived at Highpoint South prison some three months earlier. He placed his bag on the floor and as it was not fully zipped up I could see several pieces of shiny metal inside. I found out soon that all the hardware inside this bag was to keep me restrained.

The second officer looked at me, looked at the picture and remarked: 'You've had your hair cut and you look as if you have lost weight and I must say, you look much younger.' As I did not reply he went on: 'We are going to do a strip search and soon you and my officers will be on your way.'

First officer: 'Stand up, take your coat off, put it on the chair and then take your shirt off.' I did so quietly.

'Glasses, black belt, watch…' The second officer bellowed: 'You should have left that behind, your watch: prison rules.'

'But I have been allowed to wear it in prison, so why can't I continue to wear it?' I reminded him.

They both went on to explain that inmates were not allowed to wear watches on trips outside the prison because if a prisoner managed to escape, he should not be able to tell the time of his escape.

'I find that absurd,' said the first officer, and I felt a sense of reassurance that even the people charged with enforcing prison rules sometimes found them incomprehensible. 'I think Mr Sellu ought to be allowed to continue to wear his watch,' he continued. They both agreed. They searched my coat and shirt thoroughly and all they found were my cell door key, my prison card and some tissues.

'I will take your key and your card and I will put them in this compartment of my bag. Remind me to return them when we get back. You can keep the tissues.' The first officer zipped up his bag and ordered: 'Put your shirt on and take your shoes, socks and trousers off.' I did. They took a shoe each, shook it and turned it upside down. I was asked to turn my socks inside out and my jeans were thoroughly searched.

'Now hold your arms out, fingers apart, and do a pirouette,' commanded the first officer as he drew an imaginary horizontal circle in the air with his right index finger. I turned around slowly and as I reached 180 degrees and was facing the wall, he said: 'Stop there, bend your left knee so I can see the sole of your foot.' It was like being in a ballet class except I was not agile enough to remain vertical without holding onto the chair for support. 'An easy place to hide things,' he went on to explain. 'Now do the same with your right knee.' I hope I am allowed to put my left foot down first, I thought to myself.

'Now continue turning around and face us,' the second officer commanded. 'Pull your underpants down and give them a shake,' he continued. At least I had my shirt on and as it came down to below my groin, my modesty was covered. 'OK, you don't have to take them off completely, just far enough so we can see you are not hiding anything in them,' he relented. I was thankful for the proverbial small mercies. It was humiliating enough to be standing there with my trousers, shoes and socks off on a cold floor and my pants around my knees.

'You can pull your pants up now,' said the first officer. I was then allowed to put on my trousers, socks and trainers. 'Now take your shirt off again and hand it over.' I did, and the shirt was carefully searched a second time. He was particularly interested in the collar, which he lifted up. Nothing fell out. He handed my shirt back and as I put it on, the second officer filled in a form comprising several pages, mostly with tick marks or circles. He signed and the first officer signed lower down on the third page. I had imagined that I was being taken to the A&E department as an emergency, but prison procedures were clearly more important than my medical welfare.

The first officer picked up his bag and the metals inside rattled. 'Stay here and I will be back soon,' he commanded me. I sat down as they both walked out, as my left leg was now aching more. I commented to myself how cold and drab the room was. The door was shut and then locked with a key.

+ + +

Reception was a small room with a couch against the wall and a sphygmomanometer on the wall. My eyes lit up when I saw weighing scales. The last time I'd been able to weigh myself was in Belmarsh, some four months earlier. Thanks to prison food I felt I had lost weight, as I had to wear my belt one notch tighter. I stood on the scale and it registered 78 kg. Prison scales appeared to measure weight only in kilograms. As I had my trainers and prison coat on this time, I subtracted 3 kg and estimated that I had lost 5 kg.

A woman officer now appeared, in her early forties, and dressed in standard prison officer white shirt and black trousers. She wore a pleasant perfume that reminded me of lavender and had a stern unsmiling face. There was no introduction and I did not feel it was appropriate for me to initiate one. I was going to be in the close company of these officers for several hours and such a formality would have been pleasant and reassuring but, then again, I was only a prisoner.

'You are going to be handcuffed to my colleague and we will both be accompanying you to the hospital,' the first officer informed me. He placed his bag on the floor, took out a pair of handcuffs and instructed me to hold out my right hand. 'I have to put this on fairly tightly so you can't escape,' he said cheerily. 'If I pinch you while I put it on, I don't mean to.'

I took comfort in the small measure of humanity shown here.

I held my hand out as instructed, and the cuff was closed around my wrist. He tightened it until he verified that I could not slip my hand out of it and then locked it with a key. The other cuff of the pair was on a short chain and this was attached to the female officer's left wrist in the same fashion. A reception officer who had been watching signed the book presented to him by the first officer and I was told by the female officer to follow her outside. Some more doors and gates were opened, closed and then locked.

Outside the reception was a Volkswagen car. The female officer instructed me to follow her round to the right side of the car and then to hop inside the back. She got in after me and once she settled, the first officer shut the car door on that side. He walked around the front of the car, placed his bag on the floor in front of the front seat and took his place in the back seat on my left side.

The driver completed the paperwork and handed a form back to the first officer. He drove towards a massive security gate that was opened by a female officer on the ground and once we drove through, this gate was locked. Ahead was another gate in the perimeter fence and we were now parked in a holding area the size of a basketball court. The male officer got out, went to the gatehouse and came back after ten minutes. A female officer I had not seen before came to the car, looked inside and asked the two officers whether they had handed their keys in. I was told later that it was a serious disciplinary offence for an officer to take prison keys out of the prison. They could be copied and as they were master keys, all the locks in the prison would have to be changed at massive expense.

'Not easy when you have handcuffs on,' the first officer told me. 'As I told you earlier you are going to remain hand-cuffed throughout this journey.'*

I wondered how they justified committing two officers to escort me to hospital. There were no escapes from adult prisons in 2011 and 2012 and only two prisoners escaped

---

* The justification given by the prison for this level of restraint was public protection. Any prisoner who escapes from custody or absconds poses a potential risk to the general public and particularly to the victims of his crime. An escape is defined as gaining unlawful liberty by breaching the secure perimeter of a closed prison, namely the outside wall or boundary of the prison. If the prisoner is taken out into the community, he can also escape if he overcomes any physical restraints or the direct supervision of his escort or escorts. Absconding, on the other hand, is gaining freedom unlawfully where there are no physical restraints or direct supervision of officers. Most absconding is by category D prisoners from open prisons. The press often report (incorrectly) all escapes and absconds as escapes. Of course escapes by category A prisoners are headline national news.

from escorts during in 2014. On the other hand, there were about 110 prisoners who had absconded from open prisons during that time.

These figures were given as reasons to continue restricting prisoners in the way I was restricted, but inmates I have spoken to thought this was a deterrent to using healthcare services. A three-hour round trip to collect medications and to see a GP in a location only about a hundred metres away and with demeaning treatment at the hands of prison and healthcare staff can surely be off-putting. This is yet another reason why there have been calls to categorise prisoners soon after they have been sentenced, so that someone like me, who posed no risk to abscond or escape, can be sent to an open prison without delay.

But if I thought the journey in the car was degrading, there was worse to come.

Chapter Sixteen

The young man behind the reception window in the hospital looked up from the computer.

'We are from HMP Highpoint South,' the male officer said, as he handed over a letter in a brown envelope. 'You are expecting this prisoner.'

'Take a seat over there,' he said, as he pointed to two chairs in a short corridor just in front of the reception window as you came into the hospital. As this was right by the sliding doors to the outside, it was a prominent location for those coming to A&E and those leaving.

'The triage nurse will see you soon.'

As we sat down, I caught each pair of eyes that looked in my direction as we waited.

'I will go out and make a phone call,' the male officer announced, as he walked through the sliding doors.

This was the first time I had been left alone with the female officer. She looked smart in her well-pressed uniform. After a long period of silence, I turned to her and asked:

'Do you like your job?'

She looked at me, looked towards the reception desk and replied:

'Would you like doing a job like this?'

This was not what I expected but I was determined to find out more.

'Why do you say that?'

'It is a lousy job. Would you enjoy being verbally and sometimes physically abused almost every day?' She pondered for a moment and continued: 'This prison is so overcrowded and we are so short staffed it is a surprise no one has been killed.'

'Why do you do it? It was your choice.'

'I need the money,' she said. 'It pays the bills.'

Twenty minutes later the male officer returned and stood next to where we sat. He announced:

'We are going to be here till late tonight. Three-hour wait.'

He looked in the direction of the waiting room and went on:

'Still better than working in the prison. This is like a day out for me.'

He put his bag on the floor.

'So long as we are back there before nine; that's when I knock off.'

'Mr Salou,' called a tall nurse after forty minutes, as she looked around the main waiting room.

I tried to lift my right index finger in the air but with the handcuffs still in place I resorted to a nod and a 'Yes.'

We followed the nurse to a room off the larger waiting room full of pieces of medical equipment and boxes of medical stock and I wondered whether it also doubled as a store. I sat on the chair the nurse showed me but the officer I was handcuffed to was left standing. The furniture was rearranged to enable the nurse and the female officer also to sit down.

'Am I not entitled to have this consultation in private?' I enquired, looking first at the nurse and then at each of the officers in turn. The nurse looked at the officers and the best response was a shrug from the male officer. No one moved. After a brief pause the nurse asked me to recount my history.

'I will need to see your legs, so I can see the difference between the two sides,' the nurse suggested.

The prison jeans I was wearing were too tight around the legs for me to simply roll them up, so the only choice was to take them down. The presence of the two officers and the fact that I was handcuffed to one of them made this an awkward instruction to follow. I stood up, managed to undo my belt and the zipper on my jeans and to pull them down, all with my left hand.

'Yes, I can see both legs are swollen, the left more so than the right,' the nurse observed.

'Pitting oedema, no previous history of DVT, no pain but a little tender below the popliteal fossa,' I offered. 'I am on Amlodipine 10 mg and Bisoprolol 5 mg each daily for hypertension and Simvastatin 20 mg at night to lower my cholesterol.'

I had checked the doses prior to leaving the prison, knowing I would be asked this information. The nurse looked at the referral letter from the prison GP I had barely seen, presumably to determine whether I had a medical background.

She went on to measure my blood pressure. It was high, at 170/98. I had not taken Amlodipine for four days as it is known to cause swelling of the ankles, but this had made no difference. Moreover I was stressed by everything that had happened so far and by the possibility I had a DVT. Pulse 62 per minute. This should have been higher, given how I felt, but Bisoprolol works by lowering heart rate. Oxygen saturation 98 per cent – normal.

The nurse made no comment.

'I shall arrange for you to have blood tests and the doctor will see you when the results are available.'

I put my trousers back on and was ushered back to the waiting area. Everyone stopped what they were doing to take a look at me.

+ + +

'David Sellu,' called out the nurse.

We followed her into a room where I was instructed to lie on a couch.

'I am going to take some blood.'

'What tests am I having?' I asked.

'The doctor will discuss that with you later. Three tubes.'

I was not going to refuse the tests, but it would have been very nice to know what they were for. It is not easy taking blood from me – dark skin, not very prominent veins around the front of the elbow.

After prodding there for a while, her eyes lit up as she noticed some prominent blood vessels on the outer side of my wrist area with my palm facing upwards. She patted the area a few times but I interrupted and said:

'That is my radial artery. In some people like me, it does not run its normal course and it is displaced outwards. Aberrant radial artery, have a feel.'

'Oh yes, you are right. That's a bit dangerous where it is. Could easily be injured.'

'I have managed so far to avoid any mishaps,' I assured her.

'I will get a doctor to do your bloods. Too difficult for me.'

She disappeared and twenty minutes later a doctor arrived. She was tall, slim and had short hair and was wearing scrubs. She managed to locate a vein deep in front of my left elbow and she was getting ready to take the samples.

'What blood tests am I having?' I asked.

'Full blood count, urea and electrolytes, liver function tests, D-dimer.'

She spoke slowly, looking all the time at the request form. I was not sure whether the lack of explanation as to what these tests meant was because she had discovered I was a doctor. If not, I wonder what other prisoners would have made of this under similar circumstances. She was efficient at taking blood. First stab and three vacuum bottles were filled and within a minute or two the process was complete.

Needle out of my arm, a piece of cotton wool pressed over the puncture site before the plaster went on. We were back again in the large waiting room and this time a group of young children who had been watching the TV turned their attention to me. I felt uncomfortable and humiliated.

'Do you have a technical background?' the male officer asked me as I sat, head bowed, looking at the floor, tired of the eyes fixed on me.

'I was a consultant surgeon,' I said as I raised my head.

His ignorance explained a lot about the officers' attitude towards me. All prisoners were criminals.

'There is a campaign to have my case reviewed – it's on the internet at davidsellu.org.uk,' I added. (This has now changed to davidsellu.com.)

'Oh, I see.'

Then more silence.

No one spoke for what seemed like an eternity. How alone and self-conscious I felt; and so out of place. My wife and children did not know I was in this department being investigated for a potentially serious condition. It would have been comforting to have my family with me, but instead I was handcuffed to a prison officer, sat in silence, far from home.

+   +   +

The doctor in the cubicle was a pleasant young woman who introduced herself and asked me to recount my history. The officers saw no reason to leave the cubicle, so I simply ignored them. The doctor made no attempt to defend my right to confidentiality (a right I insisted on for the prisoner patients I treated from Wormwood Scrubs prison).

This time for my examination I would need to take off my prison jacket, my shoes and socks and my trousers, and the doctor might want to examine my abdomen and groin as well as my legs. I looked at the doctor first in the hope that she would bar the officers from the examination room and then at the officers. Not much was said but I still had my outdoor clothes on, including my jacket. The handcuff was on my right wrist, attached to the female officer's left wrist but with little slack in the link between the cuffs. The male officer opened his bag of metalwork and extracted a set of handcuffs, but this one was different. It had a long chain about six metres long with a cuff at each end. The male officer commanded me to take my left arm out of my jacket and he attached the new cuff to my left wrist. He then attached the second new corresponding cuff to the right wrist of the female officer.

'I don't mean to hurt you, but if you are pinched...'

'It is not intentional,' I finished the sentence for him.

He proceeded to remove the first set of cuffs, first from his colleague and then from me, but I was left with the cuff and chain combination I called 'Duke'. Both officers were now free to stand outside the cubicle on the other side of the curtain with the chain dangling on the floor.

With my free right hand and a slightly restrained left hand I managed to remove my coat, shoes and socks and then my trousers and lay on the couch. The examination was efficient in my view. The doctor's brief was to determine whether or not I had a DVT and the indications were that I might. One leg was more swollen than the other, neither was painful but the worse-affected calf was a little sore to touch and the D-Dimer blood test was a little raised but was in the equivocal range. The officers insisted on being back in the cubicle as soon they felt the examination was over, in case the doctor gave me any information I was forbidden to know. I was relieved that I was allowed to get dressed first.

As a DVT could not be ruled out and the imaging department was now closed for routine DVT scans, the standard treatment was to give an injection of Tinzaparin, a blood thinning agent, and to bring me back when the scanning room was open, to do the definitive test.

'When will that be?' I asked.

She looked in the direction of the male officer, who shook his head.

'Well, if it is not tomorrow,' I continued, 'then I would have to have daily injections of Tinzaparin until the scan is done.'

I had been warned not to criticise any part of the prison service in front of others, so I had to choose carefully what I said next.

'Knowing the difficulties in the healthcare centre, I am worried that I may miss my injections.'

'Leave that to us and we will see what we can do,' the male officer replied.

The tone of his voice was more of a command than reassurance. I was weighed – 80 kg (subtract five for the cuff and chain), given a Tinzaparin injection (dose depends on body weight) and ordered back to the waiting room to wait for our taxi back.

+ + +

Three and a half hours after we first presented to A&E I was in the back of the same taxi we had taken to the West Suffolk Hospital. Mercifully I had not encountered anyone I knew professionally from my medical life during the hospital visit.

The male officer got out of the car and took a sheaf of papers and his bag to the gatehouse. Soon after a female officer emerged from the gate carrying a two-metre pole and she signalled to the driver to get out of the car. The new female officer got into the driver's side, opened the dashboard, flipped through the contents, looked on the floor, lifted the floor mat and had a quick look inside all the compartments in the car. She instructed the driver to open the car bonnet. Another quick look. The new officer picked up the pole and slid it underneath the car, put it back on the ground and signed a piece of paper handed over by the taxi driver.

Bemused, I asked the officer I was chained to: 'What's all this about?'

'They are checking for drugs and other forbidden items.'

I thought to myself that this was at best a very cursory check. Surely if they were going through all the trouble they could search more thoroughly. Interestingly, the female officer I was attached to was not searched and I was not to know whether her male colleague had been either. Once we were all back in the car, the inner gate was opened, we drove through and alighted in front of the entrance to reception.

'One last search before I unlock your handcuffs and take you back to your unit.'

The process completed, the female officer went her way as I walked ahead of the male officer back to Unit 10. She did not say a word to me as she walked away.

The courtyards were empty and as we walked past the penultimate unit a voice shouted from a window: 'Get me out of this fuckin' hellhole; let me out, screw.'

A few metres on I enquired: 'What happens to me now?'

'I will leave your A&E letter with healthcare and things will be taken care of.'

As no further information was forthcoming I made no more enquiries.

'That was a nice trip. Better than being stuck in this place all day, and I am looking forward to signing off soon,' the officer added, as he rubbed the back of his hand carrying the toolbox with the palm of his free hand.

For me the day had been stressful and humiliating, and I felt a sense of relief being back at Unit 10. For the first time, this sad place felt like home after the day's events. As my evening meal (my tea), by now very cold, was handed over to me in a polystyrene container, I asked if I could phone home to let my family know what had happened today and that I'd returned to prison without a diagnosis.

'Lock-up was hours ago and phone calls are not allowed at this time. Make your way to your cell,' I was told.

Home sweet home.

I woke up several times in the night and each time I passed urine, I checked to make sure there was no blood in it. A major side effect of the blood-thinning agent I had been given was bleeding, and this is often manifest in the urine. My legs were less swollen, as I had expected, now that I had been off them and lying flat for some time. I pinched myself to reassure myself I was still alive. The biggest worry about DVT, and what makes it an emergency, is that it can lead to sudden death.

I was still alive.

The officer unlocked the cell door as usual at just after eight in the morning. I was surprised that he did not look in to make sure I was OK after I had been in the A&E department most of the previous evening. What sort of training do these offices undergo, if not in basic medical diagnosis, at least in compassion? I thought to myself.

'I am all right, officer, and thank you for asking.'

+ + +

At ten o'clock on a Saturday morning, my cell door was pushed open.

'You have ten minutes to get ready and you are coming with me. I will be waiting in the unit office.'

I knew enough by now though to guess what was going to happen. DVT is an emergency and if suspected clinically, as in my case, it should be confirmed or excluded by venous duplex scan at the earliest opportunity. I knew that scanning units opened on Saturdays and any urgent requests from the previous evening would be dealt with. This trip was almost certainly going to be to the scanning unit in the imaging department at the West Suffolk Hospital. I had also learned enough about security procedures to realise that I would not be told any of this and moreover would be prevented from making any phone calls.

I had heard accounts of other prisoners being in a similar predicament when either they or their family members had urgent news to exchange. One inmate told me that when someone died in his family it took over three days for him to get the news.

The journey back to the hospital was almost a replay of the previous evening. The officer I was handcuffed to was a man, whom I recognised from my stay on the dreaded Unit 14.

Today's trip was on a Saturday morning in the fresh morning air (outside) and the heavier morning traffic. The officers discussed their working conditions, the poor pay and the decreasing value of their salaries and pensions and the poor morale among staff. It was interesting that the female officer the evening before had said that although she did not enjoy the job, she had persevered because of the money.

When we arrived in the hospital, the first officer asked for the way to the imaging department, as I had guessed he would. I was on public parade again in the waiting area and staff, patients and visitors stopped by to have an eyeful of the spectacle of a prisoner in handcuffs. I gleaned from the conversation between the officers that the appointment was at 11 a.m. and we were there just after the hour.

Just after midday I was called into the scanning room where there was a nurse and a doctor. I was instructed to pull my jeans down – I did not have to take them or my shoes off – and to pull my underpants over to the right to expose my left groin. The officers made no attempt to leave the room.

When the doctor had finished a scan on my left leg he said there was no clot but there was only fluid under my skin. As the swelling was on both sides, albeit worse on the left, I asked if the right leg ought to be scanned as well. No, the doctor replied, the request form said to do only the left side.

The session completed, I was pleased that I did not have a DVT in my lower left leg but my legs were still puffy. I had learned by now that I would get very little information by questioning my guardians, so I got dressed and followed them back to the reception desk. The receptionist, perhaps unaware that I was to be given no direct information, instructed the officers in my full hearing that we were to proceed to a ward on the first floor.

'We have quite a backlog this morning,' the sister behind the desk on the receiving ward informed us as we arrived there.

This was more of a clinic with beds than a ward, with a waiting room, a few cubicles opening on to the waiting area, the reception desk and two toilets.

'Please take a seat there and the doctor will call you when it's your turn.'

The seats she pointed to were at the back of the waiting room and those already seated moved their knees to one side to let us through as I was pulled along. By now I was not surprised that everyone stopped what they were doing to look at me. The conversations became more subdued as I caught each pair of eyes stealing a glance in my direction from time to time.

When the doctor came into the waiting room with a stethoscope around his neck and called a name, one woman in a wheelchair was pushed into the cubicle by a man and a woman carrying two small bags followed them. I hoped this meant that there were fewer patients ahead of me than the total number of people in the waiting room. An hour or so after we arrived the tea lady wheeled her tea trolley into the waiting room and offered a drink to all the people in front of us. After the officers were served she looked at them hesitatingly and then at me, and asked if I wanted a drink. Unsure what was permitted in such circumstances, I asked the officers:

'Am I allowed to drink?'

'Yes, you are,' said the old officer.

The tea lady obliged with a cup of coffee and I was grateful for a warm drink.

'I suppose if they start offering cups of cocoa then we know we are going to be here all night,' said a lady who was soon called into the cubicle.

Another hour or so later, it was my turn, or as the reader must have guessed by now, our turn.

The doctor asked me the same questions, examined my legs, looked at my neck to see if the pressure in the veins in the neck was raised – if so, suggesting heart failure – and he listened to my chest. He looked at the computer and then at my records and told me what I already knew:

'You don't have a DVT.'

'What do you think is causing my legs to swell?'

'We have been asked to rule out a DVT and I can tell you there is no DVT. I will write to the prison doctor and if they feel it is necessary, they will refer you for further tests such as a cardiac echocardiogram.'

It was clear to me that this consultation was being drawn to a close and the shuffles by the officers suggested they too wanted to move on. I dreaded the thought of having to go through this journey again.

Outside the consulting room, I asked if I could go to the toilet. I was bursting. The officers exchanged glances and walked over to the toilet with me in tow. The handcuffs were exchanged to allow a longer chain, as had been done the previous day. My left hand was now handcuffed and I was linked to the officer. What happened next would have been hugely amusing if it wasn't so demeaning.

As I could not close the toilet door, anyone outside could see what I was doing. It was an unpleasant experience using the toilet in front of a potential audience. It gave 'pulling the chain' a whole new meaning. Any man who has tried to pee standing up, undoing the zippers on his trousers with one hand and trying not to spray all over himself will understand the problems I faced. Just as well I did not want to open my bowels or I might have ended up in a bit of a mess. I gave up washing my hands, as it was going to be a bit of a performance.

Chapter Seventeen

I was summoned to the health centre the following day, Sunday, at about 11 a.m. The hospital had not sent a letter but at least I was able to recount the events. I wondered how inmates with no medical background would have fared. I met with a pleasant nurse for a change who promised to make an appointment for me to see the doctor in a week or two, by which time she hoped the letter from the hospital would have arrived. I was back in my cell an hour and a half later following a consultation that lasted only five minutes. And that was on a Sunday morning.

Overall, I was disturbed by what I saw and experienced in terms of available healthcare in closed prisons.* Prison

---

* Prison has had a poor record for delivering healthcare (Ginn, S., Healthcare in Prisons, BMJ 2012;345:e5921). At the creation of the NHS in 1948 the prison medical service was run as a separate system and its practitioners were poorly trained and relatively few in number. The quality of the service they gave was vastly inferior to that delivered by the civilian health service. The NHS assumed formal responsibility for healthcare in prisons in England and Wales as late as 2006, even later in Scotland (2011) and Northern Ireland (2012). The primary care or GP-based service provision was largely by private companies such as Care UK, which won contracts in open competitions and were accountable to the NHS. Secondary and tertiary care were delivered by the NHS. The professed aim was to provide a health service to prisoners comparable to that given to the community.

However, as recently as October 2010, the inspector of prisons had this to say about healthcare at Highpoint:

'General healthcare services were extremely poor and needed serious and urgent attention ...

'Health services were critically understaffed, and clinics were disorganised and unsafe ...

'Pharmacy service services were chaotic. I have serious concerns about the support healthcare receives from the primary care trust. I have brought my concerns to the attention of the appropriate regulator.'

was clearly a poor place for the elderly and infirm. These Victorian buildings with their labyrinthine corridors, multiple doors and gates, narrow staircases and landings were unsuitable for people with complex social, cognitive and psychological needs, alongside their physical ones, in an over-burdened system. I could see the difficulties facing the service. The prisoners, many from low socio-economic backgrounds, put unnecessary pressure on clinic staff. I knew of inmates demanding painkillers, and it was doubtful whether most of the recipients used these medications for pain management. All inmates knew that stronger painkillers, Co-codamol and Tramadol, were opiate drugs, in the same class as morphine and heroin. These who could obtain these drugs did a brisk trade in them, exchanging them for tobacco, cannabis and other items. One problem for prison doctors was deciding when an inmate's pain was genuine and when it was being used as a means of obtaining stronger opiate-based painkillers.

Officers were inadequately trained in general healthcare and this meant that inmates with genuine physical and mental health disorders were not identified effectively. It took a long time for officers on my wing to take my swollen leg seriously; at that stage it was impossible to rule out a DVT. The unit officers never cared about my welfare during the times I attended the A&E department. Their role was containment – to keep prisoners restrained and behind bars and to impose discipline. I got the feeling that a good day for some of them was a day in which no one escaped and there were no riots; any additional care was of secondary importance.

There was an outreach screening service for all the prisoners but from my observations these were not well organised. The number of inmates targeted was limited and the screening comprised checking blood pressure, pulse, weight and height and taking blood for cholesterol. The scope could be increased to include more, and younger, prisoners and blood tests could include checking blood count (anaemia could be an early sign of bowel cancer) and kidney and liver function. Screening for bowel cancer using the faecal occult blood test should be a part of this programme for prisoners older than sixty.

The need for security meant that even a visit for a simple blood pressure check took over two hours. Many inmates found this a huge impediment. The waiting rooms smelling of tobacco smoke could be policed better and made more pleasant. There were notices warning that smoking within the healthcare complex (or indeed anywhere outside cells) was a punishable offence, but they were ignored.

I found the attitudes of some of the healthcare staff unfriendly and insensitive and many inmates felt they were looked down upon. I certainly felt that way. Of course, officers were also required to enforce discipline and security, but I do not believe this duty was in any way at variance with being humane.

Being paraded in handcuffs in hospital was a powerful hindrance to a visit to the health centre when an inmate felt that a hospital visit might be needed. It is difficult to see how this can be circumvented but it should be easier to provide privacy during hospital consultations and tests. Parading inmates in handcuffs in public was the ultimate humiliation for me and I could not help feeling demeaned as a black prisoner in rural East Anglia when I was treated in this way.

I was surprised that nurses provided most or all of the on-call service at Highpoint. As far as I could figure out these were general nurses who had had no nurse-specialist training to deliver such service. Inmates I spoke to resented the fact that when the doctor was needed for an urgent problem, they could only see a nurse while the doctor was at the end of the phone. I was not impressed by my encounters with the nurse whom I saw when I presented with a possible DVT.

The concentration of a large number of highly vulnerable individuals in a confined space posed enormous risks for the spread of infections such as tuberculosis and for the dissemination of drugs. It also provided opportunities for health promotion and the uptake of healthcare facilities. The distance to the health centre was much shorter than for a comparable group of vulnerable people in the general population. It should be possible for staff to improve prisoners' access to healthcare without compromising security by getting inmates to and from the centre more quickly and reducing the physical barriers that existed.

Initiatives could be introduced by allocating a classroom in education and encouraging each prisoner to attend perhaps once every six months to learn about diseases such as hypertension, HIV, diabetes, prostate cancer and substance and alcohol abuse, and to offer appropriate screening tests. Those who attend could be given certificates and rewards on the IEP system and suitable inmates could be trained to act as mentors on such courses. Reinforcement materials such as posters and DVDs could be disseminated after the courses and prisoners could be encouraged to produce these materials.

The gym is another location for health promotion. Attendance at health promotion sessions and health consciousness sessions once every three months or so could be imposed as a condition for the privilege of using the gym.

I must add that I encountered few doctors and a small number of nurses who worked hard and showed compassion. I thank them for all their care.

+ + +

I spent most of my early days in Highpoint South in my room learning Arabic and improving on my French with the help of material sent in by my family. I had learned the Arabic alphabet and could correctly identify all the letters when they were presented randomly in sentences. Whether I was reading with the correct intonation or placing emphasis on the right syllables in the words was debatable. The problem with Arabic texts is that in the modern standard version of the language, the version used in newspapers and other publications, the short vowels are removed and only consonants and long vowels are represented. This means you have to know the language well before you can read it correctly. Unfortunately, not having a teacher or audio-visual material from which to learn meant I could not be sure about my reading.

Despite my grade 1 (the equivalent of A*) in French at 'O' level, I'd had very few opportunities to speak the language. I brushed up on the language at a brisk pace and by now felt tempted to write letters to some of the French-speaking friends who communicated with me in prison.

I also took the opportunity to write the story in this book and hoped that my manuscript would not be confiscated when I was finally discharged from prison. In addition, I put my name down to go to the gym several times a week and when not there or in my room I wandered in the courtyard outside the prison block.

One day some six weeks after I arrived on Unit 10, I got talking to an inmate, Martin, a white man in his fifties doing a long prison sentence for murder, who was employed in the library as a librarian. He told me how much he enjoyed his job and the fact that he was able to get out of the block to the education unit in the centre of the prison twice a day, five days a week. He came back to the unit at lunchtime for his meals. He was reading for a law diploma, so the library gave him the perfect environment to study and moreover he was on full pay.

He told me he had spoken to a civilian member of staff in the education block who had confided that they were looking for an inmate to be a peer mentor and he'd thought about me. (I was always amazed at the close relationship between inmates and some female members of staff, both civilians and prison officers. I witnessed intimate chats and hand holding, no doubt not intended to be in public view.) Martin asked if I would be interested. The work, he said, involved helping the classroom teacher to teach basic computer skills, word processing, spreadsheets and database management. I was well versed in these and told him I even spent years in Birmingham in the mid-eighties running my own computer courses for doctors and other healthcare staff. I told Martin I was interested.

I put in an application stating my name, prison number, unit and room number and my previous experience. Two weeks later Martin told me the head of the computer unit had asked me to see her for an interview. On the appointed day I queued up by the unit gate and was herded with the rest of the inmates attending for education to the education block.

I went through several doors at each of which I had to say who I was and what I was attending for. My name was on a list and after a tick was placed against it, I was allowed further on. There was a prison guard located outside the room with 'Computer Unit' on the door. Inside there were about ten computer stations and I could count about six inmates busy working at them. The teacher was seated in front of a terminal at the head of the class. I went up to her and she asked me to take a seat at her desk.

We had a discussion in which she asked about my knowledge of computers and of the Microsoft Office suite of programs. She told me that Martin had spoken to her about me and recommended that I would be a good peer mentor. As were talking, one of the inmates said in a loud voice:

'Miss, can you come here for a minute and tell me where the "at" sign is on the keyboard?' at the same time drawing two concentric circles in the air with his right index finger. The teacher went, came back and said to me:

'I think you can see the sorts of problems you are going to help me with. You have the job if you want it.'

I said I was keen to do the job and I was given my own workstation. In the folder on my desk were explanations about the computer department and the rules. Normally the teacher would spend a whole morning going through them, but she felt that with my knowledge, I was capable of understanding them without her intervention.

The rulebook said that each computer was loaded with all the software the inmates needed for the learning objectives that were set. The computers were fully disconnected from the internet, so there was no chance of online activity.

The Microsoft packages would be taught from scratch and a certificate would be issued at different levels of achievement for each program. Those who passed the elementary stage would be taken on for more advanced learning.

It went on to say that all inmates were expected to be at their workstations as soon as they were allowed into the classroom. Noise was to be kept at a minimum and all questions should be directed to the teacher or the peer mentor. Inmates were allowed to go to the toilet but had to get permission first. Only one inmate at a time was allowed out of the room for a toilet break. Each inmate was allowed one visit to the library for no longer than twenty minutes and those who wished to visit the library should write their names in the register at the beginning of the class. Again, only one prisoner was allowed to leave the class to go the library at any one time.

Materials printed during the course of the sessions should be placed in the individual's folder and were not to be removed from the computer room at the end of the classes. The instruction booklets were also to remain in the folders.

There was huge competition for places in computer classes, so inmates were encouraged to make the best use of their time there. The turnover of students was high and reflected the rapid changeover of prisoners in the prisons. Some students would stay for several weeks, while others would drop out quickly. This meant that each individual was at a different stage of learning and proficiency and so it was difficult to do a coordinated class with all taking part in the same lessons.

I then went on to read through preliminary exercises. I took advantage of the opportunity to improve my typing speed and accuracy at my workstation with the aid of the typing program. It was a well-structured piece of software that enabled the user to become proficient with the location of all the keys by generating random letters, numbers and notations and noting how quickly the user hit them and how accurately. Later it went on to sentences and then to whole paragraphs of text. By the end of my time at Highpoint South, I was typing accurately with a reasonable speed of 38 words per minute, for which I got a certificate. I also worked hard to improve my knowledge of Microsoft Access, the database management program that was loaded on the computer.

+ + +

One afternoon, mid session, I wanted to go to the toilet. I had to wait forty-five minutes for my turn.

I finally went to the toilet and returned to my seat in the classroom. As I was busy typing something at the keyboard, I saw an inmate return from the library. He was triumphantly holding up a book with the title *Fifty Shades of Grey;* I was surprised such a saucy book was kept in a prison library. During the break, with almost everyone present including the teacher, he opened the book to a page and decided to read aloud:

'Suddenly, he sits up and tugs my panties off and throws them on the floor. Pulling off his boxer briefs, his erection springs free…'

At this point the teacher robustly told him this was

neither the time nor the place for this and he was free to do his own reading in private. The inmate spent the whole of the rest of the session reading his book. Perhaps not surprisingly, we did not see him again in the computer class.

Drug-related matters were frequent. One inmate asked whether I knew how to grow cannabis and offered to help when I said I did not know. I politely declined his offer. Prisoners talked of the ease with which they were able to exchange drugs with other inmates.

The use of addictive painkiller drugs was widespread among prisoners. One day, Jimmy and Shane were late for class. There was a knock on the classroom door at about 3 p.m. and in they came, looking despondent.

'We had a drug raid this afternoon,' Jimmy said, sitting on the edge of the table.

'They turned my cell upside down looking for cannabis, heroin, crack cocaine, anything.'

'And painkillers,' added Shane.

'Oh, yes,' Jimmy interjected. 'I was given fifty-six Tramadol tablets on Friday last week; Friday, Saturday, Sunday –' as he raised the index finger of his left hand, then the middle finger and then the ring finger. 'Three days ago, and they asked me how much I had left.'

'How many did you have left?' I asked, as the whole class stopped to listen.

'Two.'

'How come only two?' I pressed further.

'Been taking them for my fuckin' back, innit?'

Jimmy put his hands on his back to indicate the site of his pain.

'But it's one tablet three times a day, Jimmy,' I said, looking at him. 'At that rate you should have at least forty-five left.'

'Must've chucked 'em all out by mistake…'

'All right, let's all get on with the class,' the teacher interjected as she handed out papers from the previous week's lessons.

The next day the class was full but Jimmy sat in front of his computer for a while without switching it on and clearly something was troubling him.

'I've been done for them painkillers from yesterday,' he announced.

'What do you mean "done"?' I asked, naively.

'I have been put on basic for fourteen days. Fuckin' TV has been taken away. I am locked up when I am not in education and my allowance has been reduced from £25 to £5.'

'Could've been worse! It is only for fourteen days,' the inmate next to Jimmy told him, tapping him on the shoulder. I had learned from my own experience that prison was hard enough without additional strictures along the way. Reassurances such as this are futile.

'You say that,' replied Jimmy 'but this is just another addition to this hell. I was saving £10 a week of my income for when I get out, but even that may be stopped.'

+ + +

I valued the three months or so that I worked in the computer unit at Highpoint South as they allowed me to get out of my room daily and do gainful employment. They informed me about the realities of life in prison and I hoped the experience gained as a peer mentor would help elevate my prison status to enhanced. My typing and computer skills also improved and these would come in handy later with my writing. I missed not being able to access the internet.

Chapter Eighteen

'If you think British jails are bad, you want to try German ones,' Andrew told me one morning as we were having breakfast in the kitchen.

Andrew was a white inmate in his early fifties with whom I shared a wing. He had been in some of the toughest jails in England including Belmarsh and Wandsworth for drug offences and money laundering. On his release he decided to lead a fresh life and moved to Germany to live with an uncle who had promised to keep him out of trouble. Unfortunately some old habits die hard and it was not long before Andrew was behind bars for the same offence, this time in Berlin. Halfway through his sentence he was allowed to relocate to a British prison to finish the rest of the term and I met him in Highpoint South prison.

'If you expressed any dissatisfaction with their (German) system, their attitude was that you should've thought of the consequences for your family and yourself before committing the crime.'

Andrew told me that for the same crime he was given a longer sentence and he was in confinement for twenty-three hours a day. Meals were served to them in their cells, unlike in British jails where there was a servery for which inmates queued. In Germany, he said, the inmate chose whether they were vegetarian or wanted halal meals but beyond that he was not given a menu to choose from. A trolley came at mealtimes and a pack was handed over and they returned half an hour later to collect any leftovers. Andrew judged the quality of meals in German prisons to be worse and portion sizes smaller.

Whereas in the UK at least one period of association was allocated in which all prisoners on a wing or spur could mix, even in prisons holding high-risk inmates, the process was more restricted in Germany. During the short period allocated (usually half an hour), the prisoner stayed in his cell unless he had someone he wanted to associate with and who wanted to associate with him. He would ring a bell and a guard would lead him to his companion's cell and lock the two of them inside. Once the time was up he would be led back to his cell.

Non-German prisoners were allowed one phone call lasting ten minutes a month in the prison Andrew was held. The number the prisoner wanted to call would be submitted in advance and no doubt vetted before the call was allowed. He complained several times that he was not being given the opportunity to re-engage with his family, something British jails encouraged, at least on paper.

Andrew said his German was poor and he needed an interpreter to help him communicate with the authorities but his access to interpreting services was severely restricted because of financial constraints. The British Embassy helped when they could but this was far fewer times than he needed. His German co-prisoners did not believe him when he said that conditions in British jails, stifling as they were, were better than in Germany. Foreign prisoners like him were not allowed in open prisons and he only had this privilege when his application to be transferred to a British jail was finally granted.

+ + +

Mark was born in London of Caribbean parents and was in his early fifties. He was recruited into a drug-smuggling gang when he went to visit his family in the Caribbean and as part of his mission he was assigned to Colombia. He was arrested while trying to smuggle drugs out of the country and was sentenced to a long prison sentence there.

Colombian jails, according to Mark, were more like battlefields. Prison officers carried guns to protect themselves from inmates, but so, unfortunately, did inmates. Firearms were regularly smuggled into prison and gun-related deaths there were commonplace. Inmates conducted multi-million-pound drug deals with sophisticated cartels operating outside.

Understandably Mark lived in fear of his life and did his best to steer clear of trouble. One day, Mark's sister sent him money, which was delivered to him in US dollars. It was not a huge amount but in an environment where foreign currency was highly valued, he was an obvious target. Soon word got out that he was in possession of sought-after money. He was attacked by an inmate who demanded he hand over the money. When Mark refused, he was shot in the abdomen. Mark was told that the bullet lodged near his abdominal aorta, the major blood vessels supplying the abdominal organs and taking blood down to his legs.

Had Mark not been rushed to hospital immediately he would have died. He underwent an emergency operation from which he eventually recovered. He showed me a long abdominal scar that ran from just below his breastbone down to his pubic bone in the midline. None of his family in the UK knew about his ordeal until his sister tried to contact him, worried that he had not made his customary contact for several weeks.

Mark was eventually transferred to the UK to finish his prison term. He was grateful that British jails were no comparison to other prison jurisdictions and prison officers here were armed, when necessary, with nothing more than truncheons, whistles and basic self-defence skills they had learned in the gym.

+ + +

Jack, late seventies, had been in prison for several years. It was rumoured he had committed a homicide. I first encountered him when he stopped me to ask for the direction to the laundry room and I observed his grey thinning hair and the congealed blood on his chin where he must have cut himself shaving. When I told him where the laundry room was up the stairs, he took a look at me, thanked me and wandered down one of the spurs on the ground floor past the servery. A few seconds later he turned around, walked back towards me, muttered a few words I did not understand and walked back to his cell.

One of the other inmates was now Jack's carer and would help him with tasks such as filling in menu forms, collecting meals, exchanging kit and cleaning his room. On one occasion Jack tripped while carrying his plate of food back to his cell and tipped the entire meal on the floor. The carer came to his rescue and got another helping for Jack. I often saw Jack wandering aimlessly and it is likely he could not remember the location of his cell.

In my view Jack was displaying signs of dementia and while I was not privy to the facts about his case, I wondered what the point was of keeping him in prison; how did it benefit society? I was not even sure that Jack understood why he was in prison. It was likely that when Jack was finally discharged, he would be sent to a care home in the community.

I also encountered several elderly prisoners, confined in wheelchairs, accommodated in ground-floor cells or rooms with their motorised wheelchairs maintained by the prison.

+ + +

Steve, late fifties, had been a member of an all-male biker group that organised events in various parts of the country. It was alleged that one member of the group had fallen out with the rest and the police found his dead body near the M25 motorway.

The police launched a major investigation in which several members of the group were arrested and charged with the murder. Steve was one of those convicted. He always protested his innocence but lost every battle to have his conviction overturned.

Steve and I were allowed to have the keys to our own cells. It was therefore our responsibility to open and lock the cell doors whenever we were out. Having lost several items on previous units I was very particular to lock my cell door every time I was out.

Occasionally prison officers forgot to lock cells when inmates were out and this provided an excellent opportunity for possessions to be stolen. Items that frequently went missing were those that could not easily be identified as belonging to any one prisoner and included toothpaste, skin and hair products such as shampoo and soap, jars of coffee and packets of biscuits, writing materials, TV remote controls and plugs for the washbasin.

One day I was about to lock my door as I took my plastic plate and bowl to queue for food in the servery. Steve tapped my shoulder from behind and said:

'David, you have probably noticed that most occupants on this wing leave their cell doors open almost all the time when they are out.'

He turned around, pointed to other doors on the corridor and continued:

'On this wing most of us are murderers, and not thieves. There is no need for you to lock your door every time you walk out. Your belongings are entirely safe.'

It was comforting to know that my possessions were no longer at much risk of being taken. I was not so sure of my life.

Chapter Nineteen

April 2014

I had been informed that there were several open prisons that exchanged prisoners with Highpoint South and, if one chose the right moment, it was possible to persuade a willing officer to put one down for a prison that was closer to one's place of residence.

'I live in Uxbridge, just outside West London, and Springhill in Buckinghamshire is only fifty minutes by car for my family to visit,' I made my case.

'True, but buses to Springhill do not come this way often. You may have to wait a whole month for one and even when one does come there is no guarantee that there will be space for you,' the officer said in the kindest tone I had yet heard from an officer since I came to prison.

'What do you recommend?'

'I suggest you take the next bus that comes. The sooner you get out of this place the better for you and you can start planning for your discharge home.' It was revealing that someone who worked here was willing to acknowledge that another prison had more to offer inmates. 'Hollesley Bay is where I would recommend. There is a bus going there in ten days,' he said, looking at a timetable on his desk.

'OK, please can you put my name down for Hollesley Bay?'

I discovered speaking to other inmates that Hollesley was on the East Suffolk coast some 120 miles from home. This would mean a nearly three-hour journey by car each way for my family but I had no choice but to accept it as my next accommodation. I did my best to discover what lay in wait for me there especially with regard to home visits. I met an inmate who had been in prison before and seemed to know the rules, so I asked him one evening to take me through the regulations for home visits.

'You have to be in an open prison for twenty-eight days before you are allowed any outside visits,' he told me. 'Then the following Saturday you do a town visit. A town visit is when you are permitted to go to a local place no more than thirty miles from prison and return no later than four p.m.'

'And then?' I asked, excited at the prospect that at last I would be seeing places outside prison walls.

'Town visits are only at weekends and you can choose a Saturday or a Sunday. After three successful town visits, you should be eligible to go home for four nights or five days.'

'How does a town visit work?'

'You leave at about nine a.m. without taking anything at all from the prison, not even a pen or paper. You stay where you are allowed to visit and you get back before four p.m. Of course you keep out of any trouble.'

My family were keen for this information and so I tried to verify it by talking to other inmates. One thing I had learned about advice given in prison was that it varied widely depending on whom you got it from and the reality was often very different. Moreover, prison rules changed often, so nothing was ever guaranteed. Town and home visits were only allowed to prisoners in open prisons and this was veri-fied by all. The length of time spent in the open prison before a town visit varied, as did the schedules and the distance allowed from base prison during such visits. I relayed all this to my family but advised that we should wait until I arrived at Hollesley Bay and could provide them with the accurate information they needed.

+ + +

Driven there by sweatbox, I was deposited in a prison with no perimeter fences where prisoners were allowed to roam freely. There was even a main road running through the prison compound that cars from outside could drive on, with prison buildings on either side. The most striking features were the large number of cameras mounted on almost every lamp post and on top of buildings and large signs which read 'Remember keys', reminding staff not to take prison keys home.

I was instructed to take the bags with my possessions to the reception desk in a building in the middle of the prison. Every item in my possession and in my bags was thoroughly scrutinised to make sure it complied with the rules laid down for prison transfer. I had been careful not to bring anything I was not allowed or did not believe I was permitted but understood any materials disallowed would be confiscated even if they were of an entirely benign nature. This could include clothing, books, writing implements and CDs and DVDs.

Once the officer at the reception desk had finished going through my possessions and completed his paperwork I was ordered into a small clinical room at the far end of the corridor. The nurse introduced herself and took a brief medical history from me, enquiring specifically about any serious illnesses and the medications I was currently on. I told her about my trip to the West Suffolk A&E Department and the conclusion that the swelling in my left leg was not due to a DVT.

'So why are you in prison?' the nurse enquired.

I gave her a summary of my case and told her I had worked as a consultant surgeon.

'That explains why you know your medical history and your medications so well.'

She advised me to go to the healthcare centre to have my blood pressure checked as soon as possible and she handed me a sheet of A4 paper with the times I could call in during the day: 7 to 8 a.m.; 11 a.m. to 12 p.m. and 1.30 to 2 p.m. Visits to the centre outside of these times were for emergencies only or planned appointments.

I was allocated my own room on the ground floor of the induction block, a building at the farthest end of the prison from the direction we had arrived. There was a toilet in the room. From this huge building I could see the North Sea and its proximity explained why the place was so cold even at this time of year. Staff were at pains to point out that there were CCTV cameras all over the prison, including along the public roads, and it was strictly forbidden for any prisoner to enter another accommodation block other than the one to which he belonged. Even though the prison was on a public road, the public were not allowed in any part of the prison or its grounds. I noted that rooms, even though not much bigger than the ones at Highpoint, were no longer referred to as cells, presumably to reflect the greater freedom now afforded to prisoners. The last occupant had clearly not bothered to clean the room and there were stains on the walls and floor, in the toilet bowl and the sink. Even though I was going to be moved from here within the next week or two, I set about cleaning it as best I could. I got a standard pack of bedding but I noted as I made the bed that the covers were meagre, so I knew I had to prepare myself for cold nights.

The communal area of the unit had a dining room adjacent to the hotplate and when I collected my meal that evening, I sat at a table with other inmates and we had conversations about various aspects of prison life. This was the first time I had not been forced to eat in my cell or room.

+ + +

Roll call was at 7:30 a.m. I was reminded that this was a working prison and I had to register for a job within the unit. The options were few and included cleaning the floors, sweeping the areas around the building and operating the machines to launder other inmates' clothes. The prison was overcrowded and I had been warned that there was a dearth of jobs. I was shown the room where induction would take place later that day but I had to start work immediately, if I could find something to do.

I reported to the foreman, another prisoner, a muscular white man covered in tattoos. One thing that struck me as I looked around was that whereas in the closed prisons I had been to there was a high proportion of ethnic minority prisoners, in this prison there were far fewer of them. I was to discover later that one possible explanation was that the applications for white inmates to be transferred to open prisons were looked upon more favourably. Moreover, ethnic minority prisoners on the whole had longer sentences and were therefore kept in closed prisons longer.

The foreman did not say much to me, simply asking my name, prison and room number.

'For the next seven days, I want you to sweep the drive that leads from the road to the front of the building. I don't want any bullshit and I will inspect it when you have finished. The brooms and dustpans are in the store room over there.'

The area in question was big enough to take up to ten cars parked end to end and was covered with leaves, scraps of paper and cigarette ends. I spent about an hour and a half and when I finished I thought the ground was spotless.

'Not fuckin' bad,' was the assessment from the foreman, and he said to come again the next day. I went back to my room, had breakfast from the pack I was given at reception and prepared for induction later that morning.

+ + +

I had been informed that induction at Hollesley Bay covered matters relating to home visits, something I was not permitted during my stay in the previous two prisons, so I was keen to hear what the officers had to say. I was allowed to bring in my notebook and a pen and I took copious notes. Some of the twenty or so people in the room were prisoners who had been there for some time and had been recruited to be mentors to new prisoners on all matters relating to induction.

'There are several new abbreviations and acronyms you have to get used to that you may not have come across until now,' the young officer doing the induction said to our group. 'Insofar as release from this prison is concerned the most important are RDR, ROR, ROTL and FLED date.'

I scribbled away as he spoke, making sure I did not miss anything, as I had been told that these would be important when it came to making applications for home leave.

'I will start with FLED first. It stands for Full Licence Eligibility Date and it is reached when you have served a quarter of your whole sentence. So if your sentence is four years, you will reach your FLED when you have served one full year.'

'Why is that important?' asked an inmate at the back of the class.

'Because you will only be allowed town visits or temporary home leave after you have reached this date. But there are other conditions now in operation.'

We were all silent as he continued.

'You must have been in this prison, Hollesley Bay, for a full three months before you are allowed town visits or home leave.'

There was consternation in the room and each inmate was looking around for a reaction from others.

'But guv, I was told in my last prison that we have to be here for only twenty-eight days, and not three months, to be eligible,' I put my hand up and said.

'May have been so, but rules keep changing. You should not listen to any crap you hear. There are people in Whitehall who think they know how best to run prisons and we have to pick up the pieces after they constantly change the rules.'

It was obvious that there were more conditions to be announced.

'Which brings me to my next abbreviation, ROTL. This stands for Release on Temporary Licence and it is pronounced "rottle" as in "bottle". This is the licence you need to get before you are allowed off these premises. You now have to each sit in front of a board comprising two or three officers, of whom one is the governor or deputy.'

'I hear board meetings are places where people shit all over you,' someone said behind me. I was not sure if it was meant for the hearing of the officer.

'You do not automatically get a ROTL.' It was clear that we were expected to begin to get used to these acronyms. 'You have to satisfy the board that your release will serve a useful purpose and you will re-establish useful family ties.'

'But how do we do that in a meeting?' someone asked.

'That is something you have to begin to think about now. Moving on, RDR or Resettlement Day Release is the official term for town visit and ROR or Resettlement Overnight Release is home leave.' The officer was keen to finish this part of the talk. 'Prisoners on the basic regime are allowed two town visits a month and those who are standard or enhanced are permitted four visits.'

The officer continued: 'When on town visit you must stay within a forty-mile radius of the prison. After four successful town visits you will be considered for home leave once every month. The first home visit will be for two nights and three days, and later ones will be for three nights and four days.'

The rules were getting more complicated. I continued to take notes to help me remember the important points that were being made and we were told that there were extra booklets in the packs we were handed before the class.

'Town visits are always on Saturdays and Sundays from nine a.m. to four thirty p.m. You will need to be picked up by the person you have nominated on your application and we will need the car registration details. You must hand in your application at least six weeks before the date you intend to take leave.

'There is more in the packs you have been handed and if there is any specific information on matters not covered you will have to talk to your personal officers. Also, some inmates on this induction unit who arrived before you have been trained to be peer mentors in various aspects of prison routines. They too should be able to help. Any questions?'

It was nearly time for a break, so there were no further discussions, but I knew that there were important matters not covered. No doubt I would find out more about them as I went along.

By the end of the meeting, I realised that I either had to find permanent work or I could choose to declare myself retired. In the latter case, I would get minimal remuneration but would have the whole day more or less free to do as I pleased, within the confines of the prison, so long as I adhered to the rules.

+ + +

I was keen to start using the gym, which was past the library, Wilford Unit and the administration block. One important difference between this gym and the one at Highpoint was that the door was always open during the day. At Highpoint we had queued, or rather congregated, outside until the group doing a session was counted, some searched and all discharged from the back entrance. There, once we were released from the gym, we were expected to head straight back to our cells. Here we were shown into the induction room big enough to hold about thirty people. Then followed a PowerPoint presentation on the rules, the facilities and the equipment available, and how to use them. First there was what was referred to as cardiovascular exercise equipment:

treadmills, rowing machines, exercise bikes and cross train-ers. Then there were team activities including badminton, tennis, volleyball, basketball, five-a-side football and cricket. Weight training was available but there were no free weights, presumably because they could be used as weapons. Activities held outside were eleven-a-side football, tennis (two tennis courts) and cricket and circuit classes. I was particularly interested in 'Insanity' classes, which were held three times a week. These featured exercises that did not involve equipment or going to the gym, and included doing press-ups, jumping up and down, flexing muscles and so on.

Then followed a talk on resuscitation. Gym officers were prison officers who had gained extra qualifications in physical education and were taken off prison duties to run the gym.

'Anyone know what to do if they find someone unconscious?'

Several hands went up and a prisoner, keen to come straight to the point, said: 'Airways, breathing, circulation. ABC.'

'Well, not quite yet. Let's take things step-by-step,' said the officer. 'First you want to make sure you are working in a safe environment,' he added. 'You don't want to be a fuckin' casualty yourself, do you?'

Good point.

'You would not want to revive someone in the middle of the M1 motorway, for example, with traffic still running, would you?' He looked around the room to make sure we were all awake. 'What next?'

'Mouth-to-mouth,' volunteered another participant.

'Nobody does that sort of shit anymore with adults, only with babies, but I'll tell you more about that in a moment.

Next you want to make sure the subject actually needs to be revived. After all if you find him on the road underneath a car, he may be trying to repair the car, so call him, shake him or pinch him, to see if you have a response.'

He walked around the desk and sat down.

'And if you don't get a response, watch the chest to see if it is moving and put your ear to the mouth at the same time.' He paused again, then continued:

'It only takes half a minute and you know you have a dead person on your hands. What now?'

'Start pressing on the chest,' another inmate and said.

'No fuckin' chance. You must get help immediately. Get someone to phone for an ambulance. The chances of reviving someone with chest compression only are only six per cent. You need a defib. With a defib you have more than a seventy per cent chance and also you have expert help. Anyone know how to do chest compression?'

'"Staying Alive" by the Bee Gees,' came the reply from the class.

'That's right. A hundred compressions per minute, here, like this,' he demonstrated by pointing to the middle of his chest and using the table top. He placed both palms down with the left one on top.

'Little different with babies. Give it a couple of breaths and then use your index and middle fingers like this,' he placed these two fingers on the table top.

'You said something about deep fib. How does that work?' enquired an inmate.

'The thing is easy to use. Just open the box and everything you need to know is clearly written. Where to place the pads and how much charge to give. Dead easy to use,' forgetting that some of the inmates did not know how to read or write.

He continued:

'Once you revive the person, you need to put them in the recovery position. Roll 'em on their side with the leg they are lying on straight and the other leg bent. You can do this easily even with a heavy person. Just stand to one side and put two hands on them and pull towards you as you roll them facing away from you.'

He stood up again, looked around the class and asked: 'Any questions?'

As there were no questions, we were taken on a tour of the gym.

+ + +

Immediately beyond the check-in area was a weighing machine with a height measurer and facilities to calculate body mass index. At Highpoint someone had stolen the batteries out of the electronic weighing machine and while I was there I was never able to weigh myself in the gym. I took advantage of the scales in the health centre when I was allowed there or had an appointment with the GP or nurse where I could nip quickly on the scale to weigh myself. All the scales recorded weight in kilograms, so my family sent me a conversion table to enable me to convert my weight to stones and pounds.

Again, I was interested in using the cardiovascular room, dividing my time almost equally between a treadmill and an exercise bicycle, with a five-minute break in the middle. On the treadmill I was able to feed in my weight, age, the speed I wanted to exercise at and the maximum pulse rate I wished to achieve. The machine adjusted the elevation of the platform to the desired pulse rate and if the latter was consistently exceeded, the speed of walking, jogging or running was reduced. At the end of each exercise routine the machine displayed the total time on the activity, the number of calories burned, the distance covered and the average pulse rate over the time. I managed to burn 300 calories in the twenty-five minute session, envious of the younger, more athletic inmates who were expending two or three times more during the same time.

I now attended six days a week and I always looked forward to the sessions. This was an open prison, so I could go to the gym without hindrance from officers on the unit, and the facility was close by.

Chapter Twenty

As part of the induction process, every prisoner met up with a senior prison officer to review their progress and take advice on their future. A list appeared on the notice board telling me the date and time of my meeting with my personal officer.

'Come in and sit down, Mr Sellu,' he said, when I knocked on the door.

The official was a man in his late fifties and had bothered to read up on the background to my case and reports from my previous two prisons. He enquired how I was getting on and whether I understood fully how things worked in Hollesley Bay. I told him I still had no idea which unit I would be going to or what I would be doing with my time. He noted that my IEP was still only standard and when I explained that I had complied with all prison regulations and been a peer mentor in the computer room in Highpoint South, he offered to elevate my status.

'The reports say you kept out of trouble in Belmarsh and Highpoint South. You are now enhanced,' he smiled.

He explained that there were a number of units I could go to, but he recommended Samford, the 'older persons' wing', which held only about fifteen inmates, was clean, quieter, had its own recreational facilities and was hugely sought after. There were no vacancies there at the time but he would send me to Wilford and when a room was vacated he would strongly recommend me for Samford.

+ + +

I was on the induction unit for ten days. On the last day a notice appeared on the board informing us that a number of inmates, including me, would be moving to Wilford Unit. We were instructed to clean and vacate our present rooms and bring our bags to the front entrance at ten the next morning where there would be a minibus to transport us.

I had already walked around most of the sprawling prison and I knew where Wilford was. It was in the centre of the prison next to the administrative blocks and close to the library. The spacious dining room was on the left as we entered and the unit office was on the right. There were corridors and a staircase leading from here to the rooms and the recreation hall. We waited about half an hour and each of us was called into the office. There was a large board on the wall with the names of all inmates, their prison and room numbers and in many cases but not all, their discharge dates. Their crimes were not advertised.

The officer behind the desk did not introduce himself but asked for my name and prison number. When I answered he got up, took a key from among the keys on hooks on the wall and handed it to me. The number on the key corresponded to that on the label above the room. He instructed me that each time I was about to leave the unit I was required to hang the key on the correct hook. That way they knew who was in or out of the unit at any given time. He also informed me that the names of inmates who received mail on a given day would be written on a board outside the office together with the number of letters. The inmate was to wait outside the office door to be handed the mail. He told me my room, a single, was on the first floor. I went upstairs, made my bed and wrote some letters, which I could place in the postbox in reception when I came down.

The phone on my corridor was located just a few doors away and I was amazed that unlike at previous prisons, there was no one making calls. I had credit on my phone allowance so I made a quick call home to inform Catherine that I had been moved to a new unit. She said she and three of the children would like to visit that weekend and could I submit a visiting order. When I went down to post the letters I obtained a blank VO, which I completed and handed in. My name was on the mail board with the number '3' against it and I collected my three letters from the office. I always looked forward to receiving letters with news about my family and friends and there were always messages of encouragement and support.

I took the opportunity to explore. As in other prisons, each room had a card in a holder with the name and prison number of each occupant. The recreation room, which was in the centre of the unit on the first floor, had a snooker table and table tennis tables and a television. The washroom, a few doors away, had about a dozen shower rooms and I was surprised that some inmates were showering in the middle of the day. In the other prisons, this activity was strictly reserved for the time allocated for association. The laundry was downstairs and next to it a broom cupboard with materials to clean the rooms and corridors. One thing I had not seen before was a room with about six mobility scooters that were charging. It was clear that there were a number of disabled or infirm prisoners on this unit.

There were several noticeboards with different notices. On one, for instance, there was information about the characteristics of the prison population: their nationalities, religions, their ages and the locations of their homes in the United Kingdom. I was interested to note that there were prisoners from as far away as Africa, Russia, Australia, the Caribbean, South America and South-East Asia. Prisoners who identified their religion as Christian were the most numerous, followed by Muslims, but there were those from many other faiths including Hindus, Buddhists and Jews.

The catering committee issued questionnaires three or four times a year and the results of the last enquiry were on the board. Many rated the quality of the food as good but a significant number were dissatisfied with what was offered. A small number of respondents complained about the chicken portions sometimes being served with feathers on them.

Having had a walk around the accommodation corridor earlier that day and seeing the large number of inmates queuing for their meals, the extent of overcrowding in the prison became apparent to me. How could so many people be accommodated in such a small space? I did not know how many prison officials were on duty that day but after looking in the only places they could be, namely the office and the dining room, I could only see three of them.

Severe shortages of staff in overpopulated prisons was something people talked about a great deal during my time behind bars.

I shook hands with several individuals and reminded myself that I had to learn many new names fast. Many of them handed Tupperware boxes with lids to the servers to have their meals dished into. These containers could be bought through the canteen system and had the advantage that they kept the food warm for longer and were easier to transport. Although some inmates ate in small groups in the dining room, many took their meals to their rooms. I ate in my room, as I could rush back once I was served to watch the remainder of the programme, *The Chase*, which started at five.

+ + +

I was accepted on the enhanced unit, Samford, within four weeks of leaving the induction unit, with strings attached. The inmate whose room I was moving into was the unit cleaner and the condition of my transfer was that I would be obliged to take his job. This was the best unit in the whole prison and I accepted without hesitation. Samford was bound by two roads that ran through the prison and was located opposite Wilford. It comprised a building with fifteen single rooms, shower rooms, a kitchen with a microwave oven and a washing machine, a room with a phone and a storeroom for cleaning equipment. Within the grounds of this unit was a large garden divided into allotments with ample facilities to grow a wide variety of vegetables. One of the proprietors of a company, Greener Growth, which owned a garden centre in Norwich, came to the prison as a volunteer to teach inmates all aspects of gardening and they even donated equipment, seeds and plants for the prison allotments. Inmates were allowed to harvest the crops and cook them in the microwaves for personal consumption.

One of the older inmates welcomed my arrival and saw it as an opportunity to hand over his allotment, which was getting too difficult for him to tend. I welcomed this and now went there during the day to tackle the weeds. I knew I had my work cut out.

Cleaning the unit included the showers and the toilets. This was a step down from being a consultant colorectal surgeon but the job kept me physically active and did not involve travelling anywhere. Some inmates had paid jobs outside the prison, some as far away as Ipswich. Some had their own cars or motorbikes and drove themselves to work. Others were taken by prison transport. They were all searched before they left the prison and on their return. Every prisoner was obliged to pass a mandatory drug test before being allowed to obtain work outside the prison.

I spent the afternoons writing and working on my languages, as I had done in Wilford. Whenever necessary, I would go along to the health centre for my health checks, a ten-minute walk.

Did this freedom to wander to the healthcare unit almost without restriction encourage a more reckless use of the facility when compared to Highpoint, a closed prison? This was a question I was determined to ask the staff there and I would also canvass the opinions of prisoners about their attitudes to this liberty.

The clinic opened onto a large field to one side of which was the gym. Up several steps and inside and ahead was a waiting room with four seats. On the right as you came in was a small room from which medicines were handed for taking away. On the left was the nurses' room and the dental department. The fish tank with the ten goldfish on the corridor beside the waiting area gave an air of calm to the place.

The fact that I knew there were exactly ten goldfish shows I had spent plenty of time there waiting to see a doctor or nurse. The doctors' consulting rooms were upstairs, as was the toilet. The notice said the toilet was not to be used under any circumstances by inmates, a reminder not to take water pills prior to coming here. I suppose many other establishments restrict the use of their toilets to members of staff.

It was 10.30 a.m. (I usually came half an hour early) and most inmates were at work but, even so, the waiting room was not as crowded as I had expected given the size of the prison. Inmates kept disappearing into the room behind the waiting area further down the corridor and it took me some time to realise they were collecting controlled medications such as Tramadol and Methadone. As I have mentioned earlier these medications can only be given one dose at a time and nursing staff had to ensure each tablet was taken with water in a small plastic cup. Several inmates would come out of the room, take the tablets out of their mouths and wrap them in a piece of tissue paper and walk out. I was told that each pill could be exchanged for other drugs or tobacco even after they had been in someone else's mouth.

Nurses did the initial assessments and triage of inmates presenting to the health centre. The lack of a booking system to see the nurses created chaos in the system. Inmates would come to the waiting room and barge into the nurses' room out of turn, sometimes even when someone else was having a consultation. I soon learned, after waiting for nearly an hour, to be more assertive when I came to have my blood pressure checked. However, I was reluctant to pick an argument with people seemingly stronger than me, so I did not prevent them from throwing their weight about when I was ahead of them in the queue.

The clinic was clean, no one was smoking, and the staff were polite and efficient. The inmates singled out one or two staff members there for praise. The nurses' duties also included administrative tasks such as signing inmates as being fit to go on home leave and final discharge. The inmates were also required to report to the healthcare centre to be verified as having no medical problems on their return from home leave. Most inmates felt this checking out and in was a complete waste of time and simply imposed unnecessary work on the nurses. This check was nothing more than a cursory look at the inmates in most cases and occasionally asking them if they had any problems to report. The nurses also gave advice on sexually transmitted diseases including hepatitis, and performed immunisations.

The male doctor I first saw was a young man whose attitude reminded me of the doctor I had seen at Highpoint when I complained of swollen legs. In the consulting room, as was routine, I found two nurses as well as the doctor. The role of the nurses, it appeared, was to protect the doctor from attack by an inmate. They didn't leave the room when I entered and the doctor did not ask my permission for them to remain.

'My blood pressure is not being controlled by the two lots of medications I am taking. Moreover, my legs are still swollen and my suspicion is that this is due to the medications,' I volunteered to the doctor who was looking at the computer screen.

'You are taking your medications I prescribed, I hope,' he said, almost accusingly.

'I stopped taking the Amlodipine for about three days when the swelling was being investigated but I have gone back on it now in full dose.'

'Well, many of these drugs cause side effects and you are just going to have to live with them if you want your blood pressure treated.'

'I would be happy to accept the side effects if the drugs were working, but they are not.'

'Carry on with them for a little while longer, continue having your blood pressure checked and come and see me again in a month,' was his parting advice.

One of the male nurses was aware of my exasperation and when I came back to have my blood pressure measured, said, 'I can see you were not happy with that last consultation. I can make an appointment for you to see Dr Crockett next week, if you wish.'

'Yes, please,' I entreated.

+ + +

Dr Lindsay Crockett saw me the following week. Young, well dressed and eloquent, she asked me to take a seat, swivelled her chair round so she was facing me and introduced herself.

'I am afraid I have to have my two nursing colleagues sit with me during consultations. Prison rules. I hope you do not mind,' she said apologetically.

'I don't mind.'

'I have been reading your notes and I see you are a doctor.'

Dr Crockett listened sympathetically as I explained why I was in prison and I summarised my medical condition.

'I heard about your case and I must admit the medical world was shocked by your imprisonment,' she said, to my surprise. 'We will do all we can to support you through this difficult time.'

I could not have wished for better treatment. The doctor had a reasoned discussion with me about the choice of medications, compliant with National Institute for Health and

Care Excellence (NICE) guidelines. NICE is an NHS body set up with the remit to reduce variations in the availability and quality of treatments and care within the health service. One of its tasks is to give advice on the most appropriate and cost-effective treatments for various conditions using evidence-based research.

It would take about two months for my blood pressure to come down, during which time I would visit the health centre once or twice a week for blood pressure checks. One day I went to collect my medications. They had been ordered the previous week on repeat prescription and it took two to three days to be delivered from the pharmacy in Watford. I took my ID card with me as, understandably, the staff in the centre were not permitted to hand over medications without the recipient showing valid identification. The healthcare assistant who gave out the medication sat in the small office that doubled as a dispensary and was doing paperwork when I knocked on the window of the hatch. I told her I had come to get my medications and showed my card.

'We only give out medications between seven and eight in the morning and between two forty-five p.m. and four fifteen p.m. Monday to Friday and seven p.m. to eight p.m. at weekends.' I had arrived at 11 a.m.

'I didn't know that, I'm sorry,' I replied but, before I could say any more, she handed me a printed sheet with this information.

'Come back in the afternoon, I am busy,' she added.

'But it only takes two minutes or less for you to give me these tablets, I know they are in that cupboard I can see over there,' I said.

'They probably are, but I don't have the time right now.'

If there were rules governing the distribution of medications, they were unclear to me and I was sure some discretion on her part would have saved me making another journey back in the afternoon and could have painted her and the service as more caring. She gave me the package when I called back at 4 p.m.

On another occasion I made the mistake of taking a powerful water tablet before visiting the health centre. I desperately wanted to go to the toilet to pass water, having been waiting half an hour, but was told that under no circumstances were inmates allowed to use staff toilets in the health centre. I was bursting to go. I barely made it to the gym in time.

+ + +

I give Dr Lindsay Crockett and her team at Hollesley Bay prison credit for bringing my blood pressure under control by the time I was discharged, albeit with four medications and their potential side effects. Some of the side effects I have suffered have been life changing but I am learning to live with them. The swelling of my legs largely cleared but the exact cause was never diagnosed.

Despite the health centre adopting an open door policy, I did not get the impression that prisoners significantly abused the service. Much of the demand was from those addicted to drugs and those who owned up and came forward for help were treated within the limits of the facilities available to the prison. I believe there were many more who wished to keep their drug use a secret and the challenge was to identify and treat them with compassion rather than punishment.

Overall I believe the service, provided by Care UK, was well run and those who provided it were committed and enthusiastic. It was recognised that inmates in an open prison had been screened out as being low risk and were at the last staging post before being released. It was likely also that the level and types of illness, especially mental health issues, were different from those experienced by prisoners in closed environments. To what extent the differences in demand on the two health services were largely a manifestation of the effects of these two different conditions was hard to determine.

Chapter Twenty-One

My IEP status had been elevated to 'enhanced', which meant that the number of visits I was allowed increased to one every weekend. If the visitors' forms were handed in by lunchtime on Wednesday, the visit was practically guaranteed that weekend. Unlike at Belmarsh and Highpoint visitors did not have to ring the prison beforehand to confirm the visit. As Hollesley Bay prison was scattered over such a vast area, prisoners from wings that were some distance from the visiting hall were picked up by prison van and brought to the hall. Prisoners in blocks that were just a few doors away were allowed to walk. Prisoners came in through one door and had a yellow-coloured band attached to their wrists, to differentiate them from visitors who had bands of a different colour.

The seating arrangement was similar to those at Belmarsh and Highpoint South, but the atmosphere was much more relaxed and informal. Snacks and drinks were sold in the tea bar, run by an on-site company that also taught catering to inmates; prisoners largely ran the tea bar. The house specialty, Victoria sponge cake, was popular. When the weather was good we were permitted to sit outside at the edge of the huge field overlooking the Suffolk countryside. I was proud to show my visitors the location of my allotment, although it was out of view from where we sat.

The area around the visiting centre was restricted to those inmates receiving visitors and at the end of each visit visitors were requested to leave the prison before inmates were released from the visitor centre. The idea behind this, I presumed, was to prevent visitors from handing illicit materials to inmates.

During my first weeks in an open prison, I had weekly visits from Catherine, with the children taking it in turns, as only three visitors were permitted at a time. My brother Denis and my brothers-in-law Tony and Tom also visited periodically.

After these visits I'd go and water my allotment to help ease the sense of despair that I was still in prison. I spared a thought for the many inmates I met and spoke to who did not receive any visitors.

+ + +

Inmates in open prisons are given considerable freedom, but it is incumbent upon them to use it responsibly. I heard about an inmate on one of the wings, Bosmere, easily accessible from the outside and a short drive from the main road. He had arranged to have Chinese food delivered to him several nights a week and the courier simply rode in by motorbike, handed the food through a ground floor window at a prearranged time and rode back out. Payment had been arranged through an intermediary on the outside. This practice was, of course, strictly forbidden, as it was a serious security breach and was a means by which contraband could easily be smuggled into the prison.

One day the regular courier was on holiday and the task was delegated to another who clearly had not been properly briefed and did not understand the arrangement. This new courier rode into Hollesley Bay on his first evening and had no idea where Bosmere was. However, determined to deliver the food, he searched around the prison until he saw a light in the office in one of the wings. He went over, knocked on the window and said to the officer who popped his head out:

'Where is Bosmere...?'

Not only did the inmate not get his food, he was taken away to a closed prison in the early hours of that morning for what was clearly a serious infringement of prison law.

+ + +

Yusuf was in his mid fifties and his parents had come from Turkey before the Second World War and settled in London. He was quick to admit that he was a member of a large gang supplying Class A drugs in the East End of London. This was a multi-million-pound trade that the police had been alerted to and after an extensive surveillance programme the whole operation was interrupted and all the gang members arrested. Yusuf had received a long sentence which he had served in four prisons in seven years. In the time he was in prison his wife had left him and left his two children with his mother and had emigrated to Canada. His properties were confiscated and he had no place of his own to go to on his release. His discharge date had been set for three weeks, and hence barring any last-minute glitches, he would soon be finally let out on licence.

Yusuf's room was diametrically opposite to mine and he had left the door open as he often did and had music blaring about as loudly as the TV could emit from the CD player. The CD players they sold us in prison were designed to use the speakers in the TV.

'And now, the end is here...
And so I face the final curtain...'

Sinatra sang his well-known song. Yusuf tried to sing in unison as he stood in the doorway of his prison cell. As I walked past his singing got louder and the end of the refrain followed.

'I did it my way...!' was more spoken than sung.

I stopped by my door and looked back in his direction.

'Regrets, I've had a few, but then again, too few to mention!'

The two voices continued, one almost completely out of tune. When the music stopped I walked over to him.

'Good old Sinatra,' I said, taking care not to point out the irony of the lyrics, even in jest. I did not know him well enough to feel comfortable doing so, as any such comment could be construed as being insensitive. I was in no position to judge him for having taken the decisions that landed him in prison.

'You live and learn from life,' came the reply. 'I am not sure what I'm going to do when I get out. I'm not even sure where I'm going to live, but the probation people will see to that.'

'What about drugs?'

'Oh, I don't know. Still not decided, but it is a good way to make a quick buck, don't you think?'

'You wouldn't want to be back in here again, would you?' I asked.

'Look, I've lost everything in the time I've been here. There is no more to lose innit? Wife gone, children gone, houses gone, learned no trade while I've been in here. No difference to me if I have to come back in.'

I walked back to my cell and a few moments later I came back to the door and the same song was being played again.

'And now, as tears subside, I find it all so amusing,' the voice lowered a little and the tempo slowed, so he was completely out of tune.

Then he continued singing to the end of the verse, finishing with:

'*And did it my way.*'

He jabbed his chest with his finger.

+ + +

There was no prospect of release from the first two prisons I was in. I also knew that prevailing rules dictated I would serve exactly half of my thirty-month sentence behind bars and be released home on licence at the halfway point. Naturally I welcomed any hope of temporary release during those first fifteen months.

On my new unit I submitted an application to be considered for early home release on tag, the so-called Home Detention Curfew. Under this scheme an eligible prisoner serving a thirty-month sentence could be released about four months earlier and serve those four months at home under stipulated conditions. If successful, the prisoner would be required to wear an electronic device around his ankle to monitor his movements and he would be required to spend every night at the agreed address until the order was served. I discussed this with my family, who were excited at the prospect of an early release, but as it turned out, my application was refused on the grounds that people serving a sentence for manslaughter were not eligible.

I had also applied for town and home leave but under the new regulations I had to attend a board meeting whose members I had to convince that I stood to gain from my temporary releases from prison. This meeting was clearly important and I had been warned that I could be called for it at any time without prior notice, so I gathered all the paperwork I had, verifying that I had been a peer mentor, was now a cleaner and was complying with all prison regulations. I placed them in a folder that I kept in my room.

One morning, I finished cleaning the unit, as I did every day, and was getting ready to head off to the gym when an officer knocked on my door. He informed me that I was wanted in the boardroom. I grabbed my folder and made my way over there.

There were three officers conducting the meeting and one of them, a woman, was the governor's representative. I had been warned that she was unpleasant and would do everything in her power to humiliate inmates. My first impression was that she looked as though she had slept in her uniform the previous night.

'You have put on your application that you want to be allowed to do a town visit on the twenty-sixth of July,' she bellowed at me. 'Tell the board what you propose to do that day and why this request should be granted.'

'We have not decided what we are going to do as none of us knows this part of the country at all. I suppose we will go to Ipswich, which I believe is within the allowed radius of forty miles,' I said as firmly as I could.

'That tells us nothing about how you wish to re-engage with your family and you have not mentioned anything purposeful so far,' she said.

'Well, I have kept in touch with my family through-out my imprisonment and we have kept our relationship strong. They stood by me throughout my trial and they have been visiting me every weekend. They are very supportive. I propose to continue with the engagement in our relationship.'

'You have not told us what you will and won't do. I see here that you were working as a surgeon before you came to prison. We have a reputation as a prison to uphold,' I could see she was in an aggressive mood from the way she was waving her right index finger in my direction. 'We would not want the press to know that you have been let out to roam the streets. You can just imagine the headlines: "Dr Death seen wandering in town".'

That was a hurtful statement. It was the first time in my life that I was made to feel ashamed of being a surgeon, a profession where, if you got it wrong, you could be branded a killer.

'That is an unfair comment about my position. I did not set out to hurt anyone, and I was trying my best for a sick man.'

'Well, you did not do a good job. I see here that you also applied for a tag. What makes you so sure you will get one?'

'Once again, a patient died under my care, I had no malice towards him and I had no intention for him to come to any harm. People die even with the best medical care.'

I paused before proceeding to tell them how I had a busy surgical practice in West London and an untarnished career spanning forty years. I believed I had saved many lives but had been punished on account of a single incident, which I of course accepted was a serious event.

'That was a matter between you and the courts. We are here to carry out our duties to incarcerate you and if you have any arguments about why you are here you should take that up with the law outside.' This line of argument was getting me nowhere, so I decided to address the original question about re-engagement.

'One of my sons works in Oman, in the Middle East, and he will come over as soon as I have a ROTL date. The rest of my family are in the UK. If I am granted permission he and our other children will join my wife and me at home.' I told them my son had qualified from medical school but having witnessed my difficult trial at close quarters he was so traumatised that he was undecided whether to continue as a doctor. He needed my help and encouragement to continue a medical career.

There was a long pause as they took notes and then they commanded me to wait outside. Fifteen long minutes later, I was summoned back inside.

'The board will grant you a ROTL, but under strict conditions,' the woman officer said. 'Any infringement of the rules imposed will result in this facility being withdrawn.'

Once again I felt humiliated and angry. However, I was desperate to be let out, if only for a few hours, and to be with my family, so I stayed silent.

26 July 2014

Preparations began to ensure the success of my town visit. I heard stories in the prison about leaves being cancelled for the most trivial of reasons. One inmate told me that on the day he was to be picked up by his wife and son their car would not start so they asked her brother to give them a lift to the prison. When they arrived, the visit was cancelled due to the car's registration number not being the one given, and so they had to make the three-hour journey back home again without seeing each other.

Visits to pubs or any shop or restaurant that sold alcohol were forbidden. Public places such as football matches and swimming baths were out of bounds and engaging in activities such as golf was considered elitist and also banned. Inmates were required to state where they were going to be throughout their town visit and there might be officers in plain clothes monitoring their whereabouts. We were not allowed to take any items out of prison and would be subject to severe punishment if we were caught bringing anything back. No food, no clothes, no newspapers or books; nothing.

I spoke to Catherine excitedly on the phone the night before the visit. She would drive with our daughters Amy and Sophie; they were planning to leave at 5.30 a.m. to ensure they got here before the 9 a.m. pick-up time. An officer had recommended we go to a pretty village called Aldeburgh on the Suffolk coast, as that would be 'just up my street'. Moreover, this village had one of the top ten fish and chip shops in the UK.

I was up at 6 a.m. I ironed my shirt and trousers and did not bother with breakfast but had a coffee instead. I took a shower and sat in my room reading and writing. I had to fill in a form that I had to hand in at the main gate telling the officers exactly what I was wearing that day and what I had in my possession. A belt and glasses were allowed but nothing else. Part of the reason for giving a description of what an inmate wore was that if they were to abscond, the prison authorities would be able to give the police as accurate a description as possible to help them trace the absconder. The other reason was obviously because they did not want them to return in different attire with drugs hidden in secret compartments.

At 8 a.m. I stood by a window on the unit overlooking the street my family would drive up to reach the pick-up point at the main gate. When I saw them drive in shortly afterwards, the feeling of anticipation was immeasurable. I went to the unit office and handed in my room key and waited to be called to join them. It was nearly forty-five minutes before my name was announced asking me to proceed to the main gate to be checked out.

The officer in the office took the form I had completed and read me the rules and then allowed me to join my family who were waiting in their car in the car park outside. They all jumped out of the car, we hugged and soon I was in the front seat with Catherine driving out of Hollesley Bay. This was the first time I had been in private transport for over eight months and was allowed to leave prison premises without a prison escort. I felt elated, and although I knew this would be temporary, I was happy being with my wife and daughters.

Catherine and I exchanged glances as she tried to keep her eyes on the road.

'There is my unit,' I said to them as I pointed to Samford, the unit closest to the periphery of the sprawling prison ground. 'My allotment is just behind that wall.' This was the wall closest to the road.

'It's really nice to see you, Dad,' Amy said as she put her hand on my right shoulder from the back seat. 'Have you had breakfast?'

'Just a cup of coffee, Amy, thanks.'

'I charged your mobile phone last night,' Catherine told me as she handed me the phone.

I switched it on, suddenly unable to remember the passcode. I managed to recall the code from the position of the numbers but there was no signal.

'How are you, Catherine?' I asked.

'Well, as well as can be expected under these circumstances.'

Catherine has always been careful not to sound too alarmist about life in front of our children.

'What about work?' I pressed on. I knew from regular conversations that she had found it difficult trying to juggle work, our children's welfare and our financial and other matters on her own. She had also been doing difficult work coordinating the data for the appeal against my conviction, and having to read all the painful details of the case was traumatic.

'I am doing my best, but as you know, there are numerous problems in the department.' She was silent for what seemed like several minutes and I did not say anything. 'We have been overwhelmed by a huge rise in attendances for emergency treatment,' she continued.

'The plants are doing very well in our garden at home, Dad,' Sophie said, to break the silence. 'I prepared a meal last night made almost entirely of vegetables from our garden.'

'That is one of the things I am most looking forward to when I come home. Home cooking and home-grown produce,' I told her.

'How are you, Amy, how is work?' I asked, turning to look over my shoulder.

'I have been very busy this week but I will be taking some much-needed time off in a week to sort out the car and to tidy the house.'

The conversation moved on to the welfare of family members who were not here today: Daniel in Oman, James in Manchester, my brother Denis and his family and my brothers-in-law and their families. We talked about the wonderful support of close friends and the work going on to lodge the appeal into my case. Finally, we were able to switch to small talk about things we saw on the way and to make a plan for the day.

I switched my phone on again and watched the screen struggling to download icons and messages. Two thousand emails awaited me after eight months of being in prison.

It was a beautiful July day. A deer crossed the road ahead of us on the country road. It was a great feeling for me to be out of prison premises and enjoying a period of freedom, however brief.

We went to Ipswich, which was twenty miles away, passing the entrance road to Sutton Hoo, the ancient burial site in Suffolk. We found a parking space and spent the morning wandering round the shops and the bookshops. I saw two books I liked, one for my Arabic learning programme and the other for French, and my family bought them for me. I did not have any money but Catherine had brought my credit card, though again I could not remember the PIN. In any case, my cards had been cancelled while I was behind bars. I wanted a Diet Coke but we discovered that the corner shop we were about to walk into also sold alcohol. I had to wait outside.

We had lunch in a restaurant in a department store in a busy shopping complex. I had soup and a bread roll followed by a cappuccino, all of which was delicious after months of eating prison food. It was the first time in months that I was able to select what I wanted. I had become accustomed to the taste of instant coffee. Unlike prison food, which generally ended up in the bin, I ate every bite. This reminded me of so much we take for granted as free people.

We decided to head back towards the prison soon after lunch, a journey that we knew would take no more than half an hour. I was required back at 4 p.m. and had heard tales of prisoners being stuck in the countryside when cars broke down. Any infringement of the rule to return to the prison by this time was a serious breach and could result in town and home visits being denied in future. We headed back to a beach just a mile or so from the prison and I spent the rest of the time reading the newspapers.

We took no chances and headed back just after 3 p.m. The journey lasted no more than ten minutes and soon I was in the car park saying my goodbyes. This had been a bittersweet day and I was filled with dread as I walked out of the car to the gatehouse. I told my family to wait in the car till I had been checked in, as the officers had to satisfy themselves that I had been returned in the same car that had taken me out.

Inside the gatehouse reception area, a friendly officer asked whether I had had a good time. He said it was his duty to ensure that I did not bring back anything I had not taken out and I was pleased that he trusted my reply and did not search me. I was given the all clear to go back to my unit as my family drove away, a sad moment indeed.

Chapter Twenty-Two

As I had complied with all that was required of me during that first town visit, I was allowed to go on other town visits. We had visited Aldeburgh on one occasion and on another the Ipswich marina. Even though the board had cleared the visits, I was obliged to state on each application for town release what I planned doing during this town visit, to reintegrate into family life. I wrote down that my wife and I were going to sit in a given location and plan the children's future so they would progress their careers further once I was released.

We were on the lookout for people who might be watching us as we conversed over coffee and the newspapers. Catherine always came along with different family members, depending on who was free. We had made it a rule that the children were to lead as normal a life as possible while I was in prison, but I know this was not the case. Sophie had come to live with Catherine at home and Amy visited every day. James was doing his final year in medical school but came home more often than he had ever done in the six years he had been away from home. There were no restrictions on the number of people that could take me out on day visits, but we agreed with my friends to restrict the occasions to close members of the family. My brother came sometimes and at other times it was one or other of my brothers-in-law.

+ + +

After nine months behind bars, I was allowed home on temporary leave. This had meant getting clearance from my probation officer who was tasked with visiting the house to make sure there was no reason not to go back there. Some inmates were denied home leave on the grounds that there were children residing there or that their presence posed a risk to others living in the house. I spoke to my probation officer shortly after he paid a visit to my home and he was fully satisfied that I could be allowed leave. I had already handed in my application for home leave and been cleared by the board I attended earlier.

As with every excursion out of prison there were rules to obey. I was to be picked up at 8.30 a.m. and brought back at 3.30 p.m. on the day of return. I was allowed only two nights at home the first time and then three nights on subsequent visits, subject to my complying with all regulations. I was permitted to take out small items such as a toothbrush and shaving gear and a restricted number of items of clothing, all of which I had to declare before I left. I was to return with the exact articles and each item would be checked to make sure it tallied with the inventory I gave them on leaving. I was to get clearance from the health centre that I was fit to travel out and soon after return I was to report there to be verified free of illness. I had to report to my probation officer on the day I came home to inform him that I had made it to the designated location and I had to spend all my nights in that location until I returned. I was to refrain from logging on to the internet and from engaging in all social media activities. I was not allowed to drink alcohol. It was possible the probation officer could call on me any time, day or night, to ensure I was in full compliance and any deviation from the rules could see me forcibly returned behind bars and with penalties. Home leave was not allowed during the last twenty-one days before final discharge home.

Naturally my family and I were looking forward to my homecoming and all our children were there except Daniel, who was working in Muscat. We left the prison at about 9 a.m. and stopped on the way for breakfast. The four-hour journey felt like an eternity. There were road works in progress on several stretches of the route home. We stopped briefly at the probation office and I was once again reminded of the rules governing temporary home release.

How strange it felt, turning into my driveway and seeing my house. The last time I'd been home was the day I was sentenced. Somehow the neighbouring houses on the close where we live seemed different; the whole road was eerily empty, but that was always the case in the early afternoon. I could see my car on the drive as we drove up. The battery had died as the car hadn't been driven but had been declared off road with the DVLA and the insurance suspended. (Interestingly the car insurance company did not have any problem with the fact that I was serving a prison sentence and were happy for me to resume my policy once I was out and ready to have the car back on the road.) The front lawn had been recently mown and there were fresh flowers in hanging baskets on the walls outside.

I worried about what to say to the neighbours. We knew they were aware of the problems we were going through because the case had been reported in the newspapers. They knew I was a surgeon and that, typically, I left home early and came back late. One of the neighbours brought a cake and card for our family after I went to prison and we received Christmas cards from two others, but I was not prepared to face any of them just yet.

'I will get out of the car when there is no one around and go straight into the house,' I told Catherine.

'I cannot see anyone around,' she said.

I got out and dashed straight into the house. There were decorations and balloons hanging up and messages welcoming me home. It was an emotional occasion and we were all aware that this was a short-lived visit. This was the first time in over four years, since the start of this case, that I had seen anyone in my household smile. We hugged and wiped tears from our eyes. I was offered a cup of coffee and went out into the garden to see how our allotment was doing. Sophie and Catherine had done a great job and the plants were all growing well. I was particularly impressed with the sweetcorn, the courgettes, tomatoes and spinach.

I rang my friends Ian Franklin and Paul Shapira who had been in constant touch with me in prison and always offered words of support. Ian was a consultant vascular surgeon whom I had met for the first time when I needed specialist help during an operation. The patient had cancer and unexpectedly, during operating, I'd found the cancer was stuck to a major blood vessel. At the time Ian was on call for our hospital from Charing Cross Hospital several miles away in another part of West London and I asked him to come over. I waited with the patient on the table while he travelled to my theatre. His technical skills were exemplary and the patient made a good recovery from the operation. Ian later paid for and set up a website for my appeal. Paul, now sadly deceased, was an ex-patient who had become a great friend.

We used to drink together in a pub in Ealing near his home. I told them how difficult life was behind bars.

The women had lost weight and I sensed that, like me, they had been traumatised by my experience. I had attended a victims' awareness course in prison and was made aware of the ripple effects of crime affecting the prisoner's family, the third victim. They were sleeping badly and had lost their appetites. They said they felt bitter.

This was also the first time Catherine and I had been together on our own since I went to prison. At last we had a chance to talk out of earshot of the children. She confirmed what I suspected, that the family had been traumatised and that she too was at a mental low. I knew she was a strong person and we were both optimistic that I would be out of prison soon. I tried to encourage her by telling her it was only six months, but I knew that even one more day in prison was a form of hell.

It was wonderful to be home and to sleep in my own bed. The hours passed quickly.

+ + +

While I was in prison I did not have access to the internet and it was difficult for me to use the phone. But I was keen to contact the British Medical Association, my trade union, to ask for advice on how to access the information held on me by BMI, the parent organisation that owns and runs the Clementine Churchill Hospital in case we sought to appeal my conviction in the future. I knew the BMA had a legal department that doctors I was acquainted with had used.

I rang from home and someone at the BMA in London answered the phone. 'How can I help you?'

'My name is David Sellu and I am a paid-up member of the BMA.'

I went on to inform him that I was a consultant surgeon and related the background of my case. I told him I had just come home on temporary release from prison and I explained the reasons I was ringing.

'You said you have been convicted of a crime and were in prison?' he asked brusquely.

'If you want to put it like that. I have explained the background.'

'Hang on, just for a minute. I will put you through to Subscriptions who will cancel your name from our list. Our policy is to remove all those who have been convicted of a crime from our books.'

I hung up.

I had supported the BMA for nearly forty years yet now, when I needed them most, they were going to ditch me. Had it not been for intervention from one of their top officials to whom a dear colleague later complained, this would indeed have been the case.

+ + +

The next home visit the next month, in September, was less awkward. We were now better prepared and knew the drill. My probation officer did not need to see me and I had an extra day at home. Jenny Vaughan and her husband, Matt, both friends and staunch supporters, came to our home for dinner. Jenny was a consultant neurologist with whom I had worked at Ealing Hospital. Matt was a specialist registrar in colorectal surgery.

We had a pleasant meal together and my friends assured me that they would lead my appeal. Jenny had read through my case and was by this time more familiar with the fine details than anyone else, probably even my legal team. Jenny was an ardent campaigner for justice. She had led the successful fight to stop the closure of the breast surgery unit some years earlier. She was incensed at what she saw as injustice in the hospital investigation, the charges, the trial and the prison sentence. I warned her that the task she was taking on, free of charge, was going to be time-consuming and difficult.

Matt said: 'Ever since I have known Jenny, she has been a crusader and has always got a cause to campaign for. Yours is going to be her biggest challenge. Don't worry about me and the family. We are all behind her and you.'

Jenny added: 'David, when I read the judge's sentencing remarks on your case, I did not recognise the colleague I know that he was talking about. This fired me up enough to take on this case. Also if we do not reverse this conviction, it will set a bad precedent for medicine. We do not want to work in this atmosphere of fear. We do not want to be above the law, but this is a bad law and this conviction has been a travesty.'

Having updated them on prison news, we decided not to discuss the topic again that evening unless there was something I wanted to get off my chest. The next day I went to the shops to buy James, our son, a birthday card and present. I had to borrow money for this, as my debit and credit cards had been cancelled when I went to jail. I paid this back by transferring money to the lender's account from my account, which was still active.

My brother-in-law Tom Campbell and his wife Josie came to see me on the last day. Josie, whom I had not seen since long before the trial, was too polite to comment on how much weight I had lost, mentioning only that I looked trim. Tom offered to drive me back to prison, to give Catherine a much-needed break from the long drive. The rules allowed me to be driven back to prison in a different car from the one I was collected in.

My leave home in November coincided with my birthday and I was also allowed home over Christmas. The previous year I'd spent both occasions in prison, and I would be coming out two years older after a fifteen-month spell behind bars. The whole family was together for Christmas, which would also be my final home leave before my discharge from prison – in about five weeks' time.

3 February 2015

There were several formalities to complete and I was keen to make sure I didn't leave with any items that weren't mine. Most important of all I wanted to be sure that all the paperwork for my discharge would be completed so my leaving would not be delayed by some bureaucratic bungle. I was told that there was a clause in prison law that entitled me to money for every day I was kept in beyond my prescribed discharge date, but I wasn't going to chase this.

I just wanted to be out.

I went to the unit office on several occasions and was assured that all was in order. My probation officer had provided his report confirming that he supported my homecoming. I had not broken any prison rules and I returned all the library books I had borrowed. I went to the health centre to get clearance and while there I asked for my medical records. I had been informed they did not write routinely to outside GPs to inform them of any medical episodes I had sustained or the medication I was supposed to continue to take after I left.

The administrator in charge made me doubt my ability to handle my own records. She asked me if I understood *the value of the records* and could she *trust me to hand them over to my GP*? If they got lost, the prison would not give duplicates and they would be absolved of all responsibility. Given her ignorance of my medical qualification, I felt now was not the time to inform her. I simply affirmed that I was legally entitled to the notes. I had to sign to say that I was responsible for the safe delivery of these records to my outside GP. I was also dispensed a two-week supply of my blood pressure medications with instructions to see my own GP for a check-up for continuation of my treatment.

I had been warned that if I took out any prison property that I was not entitled to have, the police would be called in and I would be charged. I had collected copious volumes of material for my French and Arabic learning and was proud to have learned how to read and write Arabic, a language I had never been taught. I also had extensive notes I had composed over the months to help me write this book and I was worried they might be confiscated.

There was a huge bin on the unit for all the clothes, shoes and bedding that I wanted to return; they would be cleaned and handed out to new arrivals. My room was to be left spotless and I spent much of the last twenty-four hours cleaning it. I had bought a number of cooking ingredients such as oil, spices and vegetables and utensils I did not want to take with me. I gave them away to friends on the unit.

I got up at about 5.30 on the morning of my final day and finished all my packing. I was going to give the room a last thorough clean. At 6 a.m. most of the people on the corridor were already up waiting to say their goodbyes. This was a touching gesture. I would definitely not miss prison but had got to know some of the inmates well and had become close friends with at least three of them. It was strange using the word *friends* to describe some of my fellow inmates but I got to like a few of them and we did confide in one another. Prison would have been a lonelier place without someone to share problems with. I refrained from judging them and felt sorry for them when I left.

From my conversations with inmates, I got the impression that when people left prison any friendship they formed with co-prisoners would not survive. I might write to one or two of them when I went home, knowing how important letters were to people behind bars. However, I was not sure if we would want to meet when they were discharged. Samir, on the other hand, had already visited my wife and daughter when he came out of prison before me and he'd brought them gifts; I was determined to go and see him on my return home.

'We don't want to see you back here anytime soon but if you have to, you know you can come to this unit any time in the future,' an inmate told me.

It took three trips to dispose of all my unwanted materials and when the time came for me to leave, I had the task of transporting two heavy boxes of papers and two bags of personal effects to the reception office. The last journey was made at 8.30 a.m., by which time most inmates had left for work. I picked up my last bags and said goodbye to anybody still there.

And I left.

My wife, son Daniel and my brother-in-law Tom were in the car park in a hire car to meet me. I waved to them and then carried on to the office.

'What have you got in those bags and boxes?' the officer asked me.

'Papers, personal effects such as trousers, shirts, under-wear, toiletries,' I responded.

'We see no reason to have to search them, so we will complete your paperwork quickly. We have an appointment for you to see your probation officer at 2 p.m. today. You must adhere to the terms of your licence and for the next fifteen months you will need to see your probation officer at regular intervals and you are not allowed to travel outside the UK. Other conditions are in this paper, which I want you to sign. You can keep a copy.'

I signed the paper without reading the conditions in detail.

'You are entitled to receive some money when you leave the prison. This is the prison allowance plus any money left in your personal account.' He paused for a minute as he tapped numbers on a calculator on the desk. 'The prison allowance is £46. Money in your personal account is what you earned when you were inside and any money your family sent you that you have not used; this is £232.94.' He turned the calcu-lator round for me to see and said: 'Total £278.94. You will get it in cash, now.'

I paused. Presumably some people on release got more money and some less, but it was not much. I knew from talking to inmates that there were those newly released who had no home to go to and this money was supposed to last them until they were able to sign up for paltry benefits, which could take up to six weeks. It was perhaps no surprise that some inmates deliberately reoffended; what good was freedom if it meant being homeless and sleeping on park benches? The prison did its best to find temporary accommodation for released inmates with nowhere to go but I understood this was often in run-down hostels.

It came as a surprise to me when one of the officers offered to help me take my boxes and bags to the car waiting some distance in the car park. Outside I embraced my family and we loaded my belongings into the boot of the large car. I was shown to the front seat, Tom got into the driver's seat and Catherine and Daniel sat in the back. We drove past the snooker room at the bottom of the garden of Samford Unit, a place I had spent many hours reading and writing. It was near the perimeter of the unit and as I took one last look behind me, I shook my head in a mixture of anger and despair. No one had gained from this punitive action.

We stopped for breakfast and I was given time to read the newspapers.

If I had had any anxieties about meeting the neighbours, they were quickly dispelled the next day when I came out to start my car. Two of them came over to greet me. They hugged me firmly and commented on how much weight I had lost. They were gracious enough to avoid questioning me on my experience and future plans, but said if there was anything they could do to help me or my family, I only had to call on them. This meant a lot.

My discharge home was the moment my family and I had dreamed about, the moment we had talked about. It had seemed so far away and yet now here it was. It was the end of prison; I had made it and survived. There were times when I had felt I would not survive. Many doctors facing the GMC do commit suicide. Now Catherine had her husband back and the children had a father. I had endured long nights and difficult days on my own. Now we could share them and lighten the pain. I could eat what I wanted and more importantly not eat if I did not feel like it and not be suspected of going on a hunger strike. I could phone whomever I wanted to phone, although of course I was aware that the authorities could use my phone records in any way they chose in future.

I could get out of the house and go shopping, to the gymnasium, drive my car and take long walks. I was no longer in a regimented environment with someone else telling me when to go to bed, eat, take exercise, wake up or attend a roll call. Bank notes, coins and credit cards felt strange, having not used them for so long. Of course, without a salary and having to pay for food, utilities and clothes I was now watching every penny I spent.

These freedoms were tinged with sadness at our loss. Until my imprisonment I had worked for over forty years and loved my job. I used to enjoy meeting so many different people every day. We encountered a number of other problems.

Our house insurance provider, if our policy was to remain valid, had to be informed of any significant change to our circumstances, including criminal convictions. When Catherine told them about my prison sentence, she was given two weeks to find alternative cover and those insurance companies that were prepared to take us on increased the premiums by more than 200 per cent.

Notwithstanding these problems, I was glad to be home with my family. My reintroduction to normal life had just begun.

It was not going to be easy, but I was going to give it my best shot.

Epilogue

I came out of prison in February 2015 but was not allowed to travel abroad till May 2016, the end of my sentence. For a thirty-month prison sentence, I had served half, or fifteen months, behind bars and would do the remainder out in the community on licence. Travel was nevertheless permitted to other destinations in the country with prior arrangement with, and the approval of, my probation officer. Travelling abroad, in particular to see my son Daniel in Oman, had been one of the things I had planned for and looked forward to since we left in 1993 after working there for many years.

I was required to see my probation officer once a month and was obliged to inform him every time I left home if I was going to stay the night elsewhere. This served as a constant reminder that I was still a prisoner. If I infringed these conditions I would be arrested and returned to prison. Catherine and I decided to go to Hayling Island for one night during the summer of 2015 and she did the booking online. My usual probation officer was away at the time, but he had informed me that he did not want me to seek permission to go away but merely to inform him where I was going, for the record. He had warned me during our previous meeting that he would be taking time off to go on holiday but would pass my case to his deputy. I rang the deputy on the morning of our proposed departure and was subjected to intense interrogation. What was my full name? What was the crime I was serving time for? Where was I going? How were we going to get there? What were the precise address and the phone number of the hotel we were going to stay in? Did we have any connections there? What were the precise day, date and time I would be returning home? And much more.

While I was in prison, a group of my friends teamed up with my family and started a long appeal process to have my conviction overturned. It was felt that I had been unfairly targeted for prosecution in such a complex case and been convicted by a jury who did not understand what they were deliberating on. Moreover, those so-called experts who had given evidence against me did not understand their remit: their duty was to be objective and judge me on the evidence against the standards of practice prevailing at the time the alleged offence took place. As my MPTS defence barrister, Mr Ian Stern QC, pointed out at the later hearing, it was not about what the expert would have done or what theoretically the ideal management would have been, but what a reasonable group of surgeons would have done in the circumstances, given the state of knowledge, the prevalent practice at the time and the resources available to them.

The Empey report, which featured prominently in this case, failed utterly to disclose systemic errors on the part of the hospital. At the time of preparing the appeal against my conviction we applied for and obtained documents and emails that had been exchanged between the investigators leading this enquiry. The clinical specialist interrogator, Mr Eccersley, sent one telling email to his colleague. It read:

Dear Mike,
    … It looks like the problem is systemic, in that DS (David Sellu) answers confirm he has difficulty getting anaesthetists …

... The challenge is to know whether the problem is systemic i.e. within CCH (Clementine Churchill Hospital) or just with DS. I suspect the latter and *we have no real knowledge of the former* [my emphasis].

My friends were not alone in fighting my case. While the press had been hostile towards me prior to this point, some papers began to express doubts about the prosecution of my case once they became aware of some of the facts in this patient's management.

We continued to fight the case and in December 2015 three judges headed by Lady Justice Heather Hallett granted me leave to appeal my conviction. The appeal was heard in the Royal Courts of Justice before the President of the Queen's Bench Division, Sir Brian Leveson and Lord Justice Irwin and Mr Justice Globe.

On 15 November 2016 my conviction was quashed. In passing judgment, the judges were critical of the prosecuting barrister, the prosecution experts and the trial judge in the conduct of the trial. As I have mentioned previously, the jury in my trial had told the judge that they did not understand what they were deliberating on, but the judge had failed to give adequate guidance on which to reach a judgment. This is what the appeal judges had to say:

'In the circumstances, we do not believe that Mr Sellu had the benefit of sufficiently detailed directions to the jury in relation to the concept of gross negligence contained within the offence of gross negligence manslaughter.'*

---

* Neutral Citation Number: [2016] EWCA Crim 1716

This travesty had taken place in the Old Bailey, the highest criminal court in the land.

The Crown Prosecution Service were given the opportunity to decide whether they wished to retry me but they wrote the next day to say that they did not. There were several reasons given in newspaper reports for why the CPS had not conducted a retrial: this case was no longer in the public interest; the family wanted to draw a line under this matter and wanted it closed; 'Mr Sellu has already served his sentence.'

One sacred tenet in English law is that one is innocent until proved guilty in a court of law. I was therefore cleared of the manslaughter of Mr Hughes and it was obviously a relief to know that I was no longer seen as a killer. As far as I know, there are only two reasons why the CPS prosecutes cases: it is in the public interest and there is a realistic prospect of a conviction. I do not recognise any of the other justifications quoted by the papers, particularly the last one about my serving my sentence. Surprisingly this was repeated by a senior lawyer from the CPS at a meeting at which I spoke at the Royal Society of Medicine in 2017. To say that I had served my sentence is a statement that implies that somehow I had been punished for something I had done wrong. I had served *a* sentence, not *my* sentence.

The CPS did not want to rerun this case because there was now no possibility that they would win, but they were not prepared to admit this. I received no apology and no compensation for wrongful imprisonment. Moreover, the CPS did not retract any of the caustic comments they had been so quick to make shortly after my conviction and imprisonment, nor did they issue any clarification that I am aware of that I was now an innocent person. Doctors were being urged to issue apologies when things went wrong, to exercise what was referred to as 'the duty of candour'. It appears that when the CPS made mistakes, they exempted themselves from this duty.

+ + +

This was not the end of the matter, however. I was summoned by the MPTS to an Interim Order Tribunal (IOT) at the beginning of February 2017 at which they would look at my GMC registration in the light of the quashing of my conviction. It was noteworthy that from the time I was charged with manslaughter and perjury in 2012 to this point, I had been suspended from the register and was therefore not permitted to practise my profession.

My solicitor wrote to warn me to expect a difficult time ahead because the expert report into my handling of Mr Hughes's case was very damning. The meeting lasted one day and after arguments by the GMC barrister and counter-arguments by mine, the tribunal restored me on the register but with stringent conditions. In effect I could start working again as a surgeon but only under close supervision, with a long list of the things I was *not* allowed to do unless my supervisor was in the room with me.

I returned to work, initially at St George's Hospital in London and later at St Mark's Hospital as an honorary consultant surgeon. It was strange going in for clinical work again after a break of nearly five years. Some things never changed: the outpatient clinics, for example, were as busy and chaotic as they were when I last worked and most people were just as pleasant. Doctors, nurses and other healthcare staff worked equally hard trying to get increasing numbers of patients through theatre with dwindling resources.

On the other hand, technology had moved forward significantly, and was now more frustrating and pervasive. There was so much reliance on computers that hospitals were completely paralysed when, as happened shortly after I returned to medical practice, the IT systems failed in several hospitals in the country, following a malicious virus attack. Manual laboratory and radiology requests were now almost completely replaced by electronic ones and in many cases the results were now also shared digitally. In my discipline of colorectal surgery, the proportion of patients having laparoscopic or keyhole surgery for abdominal problems had increased. Multidisciplinary meetings (MDTs) had all but replaced the individual as the decision maker. MDTs lasted about two hours before busy clinics back in 2012 but now they took up the whole morning.

I got the feeling that doctors were afraid to take clinical actions until they had discussed their case in an MDT, expecting perhaps that others would share the blame for any complications that occurred. There was now evidence of defensive practice, in which doctors were always looking over their shoulders in case they made mistakes and did tests and operations more to cover their own backs than for the benefit of the patients. I was told that this was because of the ever-present threat of complaints, litigation and referrals to the GMC. Such defensive practices were sometimes harmful to patients and wasted resources. Patients with dangerous conditions could be denied the choice of life-saving operations, as surgeons were fearful of being investigated in the event of a death.

But I was grateful to all the doctors and administrators who welcomed me back to doing something I had always enjoyed – surgical practice.

+ + +

As expected, the GMC decided to take my case to the MPTS for a Fitness to Practise hearing. I was finally able to sit in the same room as the GMC expert and for all the criticisms of me he came across as out of touch and was deemed an unreliable witness by the panel.

There were eleven charges and these were systemically found not proved by the panel. A long list of witnesses were called, some of whom were interviewed by video link and telephone. Two witnesses who were involved with the care of Mr Hughes had moved abroad, one to Singapore and the other to Portugal. They gave their evidence by video.

In the end I was exonerated of all blame in the management of Mr Hughes and my name restored to the medical register with all conditions removed.

+ + +

Behind bars, I had missed birthdays and anniversaries and, importantly, my son's graduation from the University of Manchester after six years of hard work. During my trial, James had been in the middle of preparing for his final examinations. Some days he would come to court all day, go back to Manchester in the evening and to lectures the next day. I was worried that this would impact adversely on his performance, but I was relieved and proud that he qualified as a doctor in the summer of 2014. He came to see me when I came home on temporary leave from prison in August 2014 and asked to talk to Catherine and me.

We were a close-knit family and I always encouraged our children to come to us with their problems, but we also allowed them to make decisions regarding the courses they wanted to do at university and the jobs they wanted to pursue. James had chosen to read medicine and it was a source of pride for me to know that he had put Manchester, my old medical school, as first choice.

Now I was home, James had something to tell me. His voice faltered at first but he went on to explain what was on his mind. He was a good speaker and came straight to the point.

'Mum, Dad, I do not want to pursue a career in medicine. I want to get out,' he said.

He was looking at Catherine and then fixed his gaze nervously on me. He did not wait for a reaction but went on to say that he had seen how humiliated I'd been during the course of the investigation and particularly the trial. In his words, I had given my entire professional life to the practice of medicine and, as he now reminded me, I'd made sacrifices, which included missing out on birthday celebrations, sports days and nativity plays. Yet, because of a single incident, my previous track record and my contribution to society in general had amounted to zero when it came to mitigating my sentence.

If this was what he could expect from the profession, then he was not prepared to start his foundation hospital training.

Catherine looked at me to say something, which I now did. I reminded James that as a twenty-four-year-old, he had spent six years in medical school, equivalent to a quarter of his life and much of the whole of his adult life. He had invested a huge amount of time and effort to his studies and he was going to be encumbered with over £80,000 of debt in the form of a student loan.

But he had made up his mind and nothing we said would change that. He later went into business and never again set foot in a hospital to work. For our part, we had no choice but to respect his decision. Medicine had lost another doctor, and we were convinced that James would have made an excellent doctor.

+ + +

Naturally there was relief that this case had finally been concluded, but why did it take eight years, during which time my life and that of my family was put on hold, resulting in lifelong psychological, financial and professional consequences? One of Mr Hughes's daughters came to parts of this hearing and I cannot imagine the anguish the family went through each time this case came up for discussion. I do not know what their reaction was to the news that I had been cleared after the events in the criminal courts.

In English law the defendant does not have to prove their innocence; it is the duty of their accuser or the prosecution and the GMC in my case to prove my guilt. The bar for this proof is considerably higher in a criminal court such as the Old Bailey than in a civil jurisdiction such as the MPTS. Here was an unjust irony: I went to prison on the charges relating to this patient's death, but was completely cleared in a civil hearing. It has since been noted that criminal courts are not the proper place to investigate complex medical matters.

A final elephant in the room. Race. Would the outcome of this case have been different if I was white?

As they say in prison, 'Was it 'cos I is black?'

That is a question for the Crown Prosecution Service, the Courts and the GMC. This question has been raised for decades and the fact that there is no acknowledgement from them that there is racial disparity in their investigations, prosecutions and punishments meted out gave me no comfort. After all that I went through, I felt the answer to the question was *Yes*. Ethnic minority doctors are still at a disadvantage in the NHS, even though this service would collapse without our contribution.

People who have followed this sad and painful story have frequently congratulated me on winning my case in the court of appeal and at the MPTS against the GMC. I quietly acknowledge these kind wishes, but this has not been a victory for me. As Lord Leveson said of my case in the court of appeal, there have been no winners. Circumstances have demonstrated that this case should never have been brought against me.

It is difficult re-starting a surgical career at my age but I am persevering in part because I have started doing voluntary work in Sierra Leone – where my story began.

Thanks to:

My wife, Catherine and our children, Amy, Daniel, Sophie and James, Daniel's wife, Hayley and Amy's fiancé, Leo Miles.

My brother Denis and family; brothers-in-law Tom and Tony Campbell and family.

Dr Jenny Vaughan and husband Mr Matt Dunckley.

Lawyers: Mr Mark Ellison QC (QEB); Mr David Emmanuel QC (Garden Court Chambers); Mr Matt Foot (Birnberg Peirce); Ms Cassandra Dighton; Mr Hugh Davies QC (Raymond Buildings); Mr Ian Stern QC (2 Bedford Row); Mr John Mitchell and Mr Simon Turner (Weightmans); Mr Andrew Truby and Ms Jane Lang (BLM).

The Medical Protection Society: Dr Rob Hendry; Dr Tom Lloyd; Dr Zaid Al-Najjar.

Friends: Mr Ian Franklin; Professor Peter Taylor; Mr Peter McDonald; Professor Roger Kirby; Dr Frank Geoghegan; Dr Miranda Harvie; Dr John Vogel; Mr David Melville; and countless others who offered support.